PRAISE FOr
"MONEY, PLAIN & SIMPLE"

"...simply the most important book I've ever read. Steven Spence carefully articulates a message that explains how the institutions behind money work and how it affects you. Steven Spence's work is on a par with the genius of DaVinci and Copernicus, heretics who proved that Earth revolves around the sun. A remarkable book both in content and timing. A 'must-read' that is an amazing guide to understanding the global monetary system and why the shine is off the U.S. dollar's position as the Gold Standard of world currencies going forward. Steven is a gifted writer and teacher and I confidently predict that *Money Plain and Simple: What the Institutions and the Elite Don't Want You to Know*, brilliantly written and argued, will become the defining book."

—**John Kerry**, *Goodreads*

"A good personal finance book is one that offers valuable information on how to manage spending, savings, debt, and investments. *Money Plain & Simple* is among the best finance books, because it does all that in a package that's also entertaining, upbeat, and accessible. You cannot beat the depth of information Steven J. Spence provides."

—*The Reviewer*

"A very well written book aimed for laypeople that will open your eyes as to what is actually happening around us (and scare the bejezus out of you in the process). I would consider this required reading for everyone (along with Robert Kiyosaki's 'Rich Dad Poor Dad' which Spence also lists as his first recommended reading). Everyone needs to realize what is going on, what will inevitably happen as a result, and start taking action now to protect yourself. The "great reset" is about to take place!"

—Paul Gruhn

"The author does a great job of really laying out the concept of banking systems, credit, and how our finances are impacted through education and detailed lessons throughout this book. The way the author interweaves their own experiences throughout their life and the way so many of us are introduced to debt through credit cards and difficulty finding reasonably paid work after education was such a great way to open up this road, and the deep dive the author took into the history and modern impact of finances on the U.S. financial system was thought-provoking."

—Anthony Avina, author, journalist and book blogger

"Giving the layman a history to fiat money, global monetary policy, Bitcoin, and more. It's a great simplistic explanation of historical changes in the banking and mining industry. The books shows the information you were taught in class, but may have missed...not really understanding the legal and political changes by laws and monetary policy."

—Theresa Hulongbayan, book blogger

"Offering his own past history of living in the flat line of income and relating his advancing into monetary knowledge guarantees that the reader will relate, and learn, following Steven's own steps to enlightenment....the fount of knowledge that this book shares, and the tone of communication that Spence uses to truly educate us about money — from the global currency as it has been and is now, to the heretofore mystical topic of cryptocurrency, bitcoin, and other high tech permutations we read about in the media but simply don't understand. In other words, this is a history lesson that begins with gold and silver, progresses through the myriad channels of manipulation in various economies, the banking system in the US, inflation, deflation, and how these influence 'money', and the transition to digitalization – of life, and of course, money. Spence makes it all understandable, and in doing so prepares us well for the future of economics and the monetary systems that are coming. Basic and helpful information and a wakeup call!"

—**Grady Harp**, an author and *Top 100 Amazon reviewer*

What the Institutions and the Elite
Don't Want You to Know

REVISED + UPDATED
2023

MONEY

$

BOOK
EXCELLENCE
AWARDS
WINNER
www.bookexcellence.com

PLAIN

&

$IMPLE

Steven J. Spence

LU☾ID
HOUSE
PUBLISHING

LU(ID
HOUSE
PUBLISHING

Published in the United States of America by Lucid House Publishing, LLC
www.LucidHousePublishing.com
Copyright © 2021 by Steven J. Spence
The 2023 updated second edition is available in print and e-book form via Lucid House Publishing, LLC.
The first edition is available in both formats in English and Spanish. It is also available as an audiobook in
conjunction with Blackstone Publishing.
Cover and interior design: Troy King
Interior formatting print and e-book: Jan Sharrow
Author's photo: Adriana Fujimoto
All rights reserved. Second edition, revised and updated March 2023.

This book was written for informational purposes only. It is of a general nature and does not address the
circumstances of any particular individual or entity. It is not intended to be a source of advice or credit analysis
with respect to the material presented. The information and/or documents contained in this book do not
constitute professional, legal, tax, investment or financial advice and should never be used without first
consulting with a financial professional to determine what may be best for your individual needs. No client or
fiduciary relationship is formed by your use of the information contained herein. You should never make any
investment decision without first consulting with your own financial advisor and conducting your own research
and due diligence. The publisher and the author do not make any guarantee or other promise as to any results
that may be obtained from using the content of this book. The publisher and the author disclaim any liability
for any loss, damage, cost or expense should any information, commentary, analysis, opinions, advice and/or
recommendations contained in this book prove to be inaccurate, incomplete, or unreliable, or result in any
investment or other financial losses, and .you agree not to hold the publisher, the author, or their affiliates liable
for any possible claim for damages arising from any decision you make based on information or other content.
You alone assume the sole responsibility of evaluating the merits and risks associated with the use of any
information contained herein before making any decisions based on such information, and your use of the
information contained in, referenced or made available in this book is at your own risk.

Library of Congress Cataloging-in-Publication Data
Name: Spence, Steven J., 1963-
Money plain & simple/what the institutions and the elite don't want you to know/Steven J. Spence
Description: First Edition/Marietta, Georgia: Lucid House Publishing, 2021
Identifiers: Library of Congress Control Number: 2021945500
ISBN 978-1-950495-38-2 (paperback)
ISBN 978-1-950495-39-9 (e-book)

Subjects: 1) Global Economy 2) Real money 3) Fiat currency 4) Financial freedom 5) Financial bondage
and debt 6) Economic theories 7) Inflation 8) Gold Standard 9) Cryptocurrency 10) Economic corruption
11) Wealth transfer 12) Resetting the Financial System 13) Financial literacy 14) Bank failures

BU3045000/Business & Economics/Money & Monetary Policy
BUS069000/Economics/General

BUS107000/Personal Success

DEDICATION

All glory and praise to Jesus Christ for leading me to the truth in all things, to include the global financial system. Without His direction, I would have never learned these truths I share in this book and, therefore, never would have written *Money Plain & Simple* to share with the world.

> "In all your ways acknowledge Him,
> and He shall direct your paths."
> —Proverbs 3:6

To my beautiful wife, Adriana, who is my frontline sounding board and my biggest fan. You have put up with hours and hours of listening, proofreading, and, most importantly, encouraging me in researching and writing *Money Plain & Simple* and making this book a success. I love you so much.

To my children Shannon, Lucas, and Rachel. I wish circumstances were different during our child- rearing years. I did not pass on these truths, because I was deceived as well and simply did not know. Now, my lessons are available to you, and I pray for your understanding and knowledge. Knowledge is power and will re-shape and guide your financial future. As I have learned, it is never too late to start any change.

"And have no fellowship with the unfruitful works of darkness, but rather expose them. For it is shameful even to speak of those things which are done by them in secret. But all things that are exposed are made manifest by the light, for whatever makes manifest is light."

— Ephesians 5: 11-13 (NKJV)

CONTENTS

INTRODUCTION

Have you ever heard the saying: *You don't know what you don't know?* For me, this statement hit home, especially when it comes to our money system.

Once I ventured out into the world to earn a living, it took me more than twenty years to stumble upon some realizations and hard truths about money. I discovered monetary practices and policies that were always there but never taught to me. After decades of relying on false assumptions and a series of painful, hard-won lessons, I finally woke up to how our monetary system really works. Ultimately, I also learned that I was not the only one who was stuck in the dark when it comes to our monetary system. Far from it. I discovered that it is really a complex and mysterious realm that only the smart bankers and investors are allowed to know about. Note the heavy sarcasm in that last sentence.

My purpose in writing **Money Plain & Simple** is to share with you what I have discovered about the money we work for, spend, and save. This is not the book that's going to tell you how to get rich quick, nor is it a "do this [insert scheme here]" action book. This is not a book on the most recent fad budgeting plan, and it's not a stock market playbook.

Instead, my goal is to educate. I want to inspire you to think about your financial freedom and to "de-mystify" the system that a lot of us are unknowingly participating in — the very system that is likely keeping you in a holding pattern when it comes to building wealth. By reading on, you will be motivated to make course corrections to your financial future. You will be empowered to take steps toward a financial future that is tailored for you and not the "one-plan-fits-all" financial plan in which we have been indoctrinated to enroll.

The topics of this book are only intended to open doors to your mind. My desire for you is that you no longer have to say, "I don't know what I don't know." Whether you realize it or not, we all exist in a global debt money system. This is an undeniable fact. Regardless of your personal financial status, you are still operating in this system that is based on indebtedness. Through the messages in this book, I aim to show you how indebtedness is bondage that has you in shackles. Knowledge is power and being armed with information puts the keys to those shackles in your hands. All you have to do is turn the key.

Once I uncovered these fundamental truths about our monetary system, I was able to make some powerful changes in how I manage my money and achieved financial freedom. But before I share the big reveal that I hope helps put you on the path financial freedom, I want you to understand that where I am today is far from where I started. Let me tell you how I got here.

I am just an average guy who immigrated to the United States as a child (American military father and German mother). My younger brother was born in the U.S. My parents divorced soon after my brother's birth. We quickly went from a low-income family to a household routinely facing financial hardships. My mother had a heavy German accent and no skills suited to employment in her new country. My father disappeared. I rarely saw him throughout my childhood, and financial support was minimal as well. Once my mother came home from her low-wage job and told me her boss had threatened to fire her that day due to her heavy accent.

Like so many households led by single moms, who live on the edge of poverty, we were evicted a couple of times. Although divorce is commonplace today, it was not nearly as common when I grew up in the 1960s and 1970s. All I knew was that our lives weren't normal compared to the families I saw all around us. We bounced around quite a bit, living with friends and family to survive. I can count thirteen different schools that I attended. I primarily attended public schools in the United States (Memphis, Tennessee, and Northern Virginia). During an especially rough patch though my mom sent my brother and me to our grandparents in Germany where we attended parts of a few elementary school years in that country. Despite all the chaos and insecurity caused by constantly changing schools and even countries, I managed to keep my grades at a C or above.

When I reached age seventeen, I joined the US Air Force with $20 in my pocket. I had few options of work after graduating in northern Virginia, and there was no hope for college at that time. I knew the military would be my best bet for a good future. During my time in the military, I enjoyed job stability, but the income was incredibly low.

Since I had steady work, I was introduced to credit cards as soon as I turned eighteen. After growing up with little to nothing, what a rush it was to go out and buy something with money that I did not have. That led to the minimum payment world and that enabled me to get another credit card. And guess what? Like the first card, I ran that to the limit, too, and quickly spent all the easy money. I always thought, *why not?* I thought as long as I could service my debt by making the minimum payments, life was good.

This behavior got me to a point of excessive debt, and trust me, with no one to stop me, I went a little crazy. So, I got myself and my family in over our heads — and as life goes, stuff happens like a car needing repairs or your child needing a $65 calculator for school. To take care of these unforeseen needs usually required money, money I did not have. I fell into the "Rob Peter to pay Paul" trap, because soon I could not afford those minimum payments of the debts I had incurred.

I still have this memory of getting that dreaded credit card bill in the mail. I habitually put the unopened envelope directly in a bill drawer to make it disappear. Temporarily, that is. I thought "out of sight, out of mind" was a good plan. The debt collectors called when the bills were overdue. I got crafty at the "robbing Peter to pay Paul" technique. This self-created fiasco went on for years, and at times, I picked up part-time work to try to pay down my debt. However, it felt like an impossible mountain to climb. It seemed to take an eternity to make any progress at all. In a nutshell, this was the first half of my adult life: work, spend, pay, repeat. Is this starting to sound at all familiar to you?

I always wondered if there was a better way. I felt trapped. In case you do not know, you cannot earn overtime in the military, your pay is fixed. Also, during my military service, it was very hard to get a promotion. At least for me! But I thought, "There had to be more to life than just this." So, at 32 years old, I went to night school and earned a bachelor's degree in Aviation Maintenance Management from Wilmington University, Delaware. I heard somewhere that if you want more money, you need to make yourself better. It sounded logical, right?

Getting that degree took me eight long years to reach that goal, and it did help me grow as a person, but not financially as I had hoped. Around the time of graduation, I was also approaching military retirement age in my late 30s. After seeing the measly amount my pension would be paying me as a retired service member, I knew I couldn't support myself on that alone, so I got a "real job" as a civilian. I accepted a flying mechanic position with an international charter airline. My boss allowed me to work overtime.

And that is what I did. I worked thirty days straight with zero days off. I was finally starting to see excess money in my bank account. I thought, *Finally. I'm going to make it.*

By this time, it was the early 2000s, and I was in my early 40s. America's housing boom was beginning, and fortunately, I made a really good profit on my single-family home in Dover, Delaware, when I sold it. I finally was debt free and started growing a 401K retirement account.

What about my personal life? I am not proud of my past, and a left out an important piece of this puzzle! I married my first wife —yes, there is more than one—at the tender age of seventeen. We had two children together. My daughter is the first born, and my son was born eight years later. We divorced, and as I have already shared, we were drowning in debt. Our split only exacerbated the financial challenges.

I fought for custody of my children and won, but a single father in the military back then was not a good recipe for military readiness. Within a couple of years, I thought would be a great idea to marry again. The second time around I married a woman with three girls. Yes, your math is correct: We had five children between us. Next we decided to move our blended family to Germany when the U.S. Air Force offered that assignment. During the two and a half years we lived overseas, we had to return to the U.S. about four times a year to bring the children back to visit with their respective fathers and mother (my ex-wife). On a return visit to the U.S., my children decided to go back to their mom. The blended family thing was not working out the way we envisioned.

From that point, our relationship began to erode, and we divorced after nine years of marriage. Can you see why I had financial problems? But wait, eight years after my second divorce was finalized, I took another trip down the aisle. Although my third wife didn't have children, my son came to live with us as a teenager. Guess what? Yup, another divorce! We split six years later.

Are you exhausted from reading this saga? I know that I am! As I write this, I recognize that my absence as a husband and a father because of working so many hours contributed to the string of broken homes I left in my wake. I only wanted to provide for my families and ended up losing them.

Despite the personal pain I struggled through and caused, I still took pride in my financial accomplishments at this point in my life. I was also still working non-stop to make it all work. I needed to keep up the crazy pace to live a so-called comfortable life and have a plan to retire. Isn't this what we all want at some point?

The only thing I knew to do was to continue working as hard as possible while I still had the body to do it. As I look back on these years now, I think, *Wow, what a sad way to live...* But this was just the way it was done. In fact, almost everyone I knew was doing about the same as I was. Some were a little better off, and some were not. Some were not thinking of the retirement plan, and some focused on having nice and expensive things. It always seemed to be a tradeoff for one or the other. It was always though trading time for money. In the United States of America, it was easy to live beyond our means. But why?

And herein lies the trap. The genius part of this trap is that it was created so that you don't realize you are in a trap. By design the debt-based monetary system and by your own blindness to its realities, you will more than likely stay in the rat race that I just described and inhabited for decades. I was the main participant, and I was there for every financial decision I made. I had no one to blame but myself.

When did things change for me? When did I start thinking differently about my financial future? When did I start questioning "the way it's always been done"? By that time, I had a ton of questions.

I finally found a well-paying job with a major defense contractor (by my standards anyway), and after seven years, the plant downsized and offered me a voluntary layoff. I accepted. The layoff came at a good time since I was already planning on a course correction for my career, because I was still not on track to meet my retirement goals. Remember, I had to make up for all the mistakes of my past, and I did not want to work into my 70s. My outlook on what was important had shifted, too. I'd become a Christian and met and married my wife Adriana, who shares my values. She has an adult daughter, who is out on her own now. We were empty nesters and took time to reevaluate where we were heading.

After researching different strategies, I decided to focus on real estate investing as a vehicle to help me achieve those goals. Adriana and I agreed that instead of getting a new job following that layoff I would pursue real estate investing full time.

No pressure, right? Especially since I'd never been an entrepreneur. I'd gone straight from the military into working for a large corporation.

Well, as I started this journey, I demanded of myself to master this new skill of real estate investing as quickly as possible. I was starting from ground zero, so I started learning as much as I could. The deeper I dove into the real estate world, the more I was introduced to another world: the financial world.

Honestly, I probably could have chosen not to enter this other world and have been fine, But as a person who always asks *Why?*, I am one of those people who wants to understand how things work. I always want to peek behind the curtain and see the wizard pulling the strings. As I studied the world of finance and how deals get made, I was amazed and astonished by the things I learned. I also realized how confusing the whole shebang was and how much easier—at least in my head—it would be to walk away from this confusing world of our monetary system and go back to what I *thought* I knew. You have this book in your hands because I am not that person. I could not "un-see" or "un-know" the things I learned about the world's financial system.

This book reveals a financial world that I had never seen before, even though it had always existed in plain sight. I will present the topics that will benefit you the most, and while this world is extremely complex, I've done my best to keep it simple. I share only the basics, only the top layer of pertinent information. But even with just the bare minimum level of information, you will soon see that the financial system is rigged.

I will also explain why **you** should know this. By the end of *Money Plain & Simple*, I anticipate that you will be intrigued by certain topics and will pursue a deeper understanding and knowledge about them. We will not be able to change the monetary system, but with this knowledge comes wisdom, and you will be better equipped to navigate around the traps that are set.

Some of you may have well-paying jobs, but when you think about it, how will you retire? Will your money be there when you need it? Will government-sponsored retirement systems cover your expenses? What about retirement plans from the companies that employ the majority of today's workforce?

Here's the hard truth. Those retirement plans are a relic of the past. The security that was once there is now unreliable or even nonexistent. Without this safety net, it's time we each step up and take control of our future. I want to show you how to get back into the driver's seat and start your journey toward financial freedom. I want to turn your focus from looking in the rearview mirror at what was and start looking ahead at the curves in the road.

This knowledge, if used correctly, will show you the exit ramp from the grind. So, let's find out what you do not know and change that. Allow me to ask you this: If you do not know the truth, how often can you be lied to? Just because you are unaware of something happening, does that mean it is not happening?

CHAPTER 1

MONEY

"It is well enough that people of the nation do not understand our banking and monetary system, for if they did, I believe there would be a revolution before tomorrow morning."
—**Henry Ford** (1863-1947), Founder of the Ford Motor Company

Have you ever thought about what money is or where it comes from? On the surface, we all know what money is in terms of cash, and we've all probably seen pictures of cash being printed on the printing presses and coins pressed out of metal slugs. But let's go a little deeper. Take into consideration the cash printing press. Does that use special paper? Does the ink have some sort of value? What about coins? Are the slugs that are pressed made of valuable metals?

And here's a bigger question: What is the purpose of the money? Well, most of us will say that money is what you buy things with at the store, or it is what you use to pay your electric bill or rent. Money is the reason you go to work—to make money. It is the common denomina¬tor for almost everything we do in our lives, in almost every part of the world. Yet, we know so little about it.

For example, where does money come from, what gives it value, why does its value change? Why do some folks have more money and others have less?

$IDE NOTE: The functions of money are: 1) a medium of exchange, 2) a unit of account and 3) a store of value. It is important to understand this as not all items that seem to be money qualify as money according to these three functions.

For the first twenty years of my adult life, it seemed that I never had any money. I could never seem to catch a break. I was usually behind on my bills, or always robbing Peter to pay Paul. Gosh, I even remember having to go to the credit union for a $100 loan when times were tight. It felt like all I could do was run faster on the hamster wheel of life. My solutions at that time always involved figuring out how to get more money. I did not know any better, as I "did not know what I did not know." I never questioned my situation, as I thought it was normal. That's just what people had to do when they grew up, right?

Well, several years ago, I started to take notice of some anomalies that were happening in the financial world. I will cover some of the details of these anomalies later. As I mentioned before, at that point, I did not have much wealth in my life, so I really didn't pay much attention then. I thought I didn't have much to lose since I mostly had just debt. Rather, the answer to my problems was to work more. Once I implemented this strategy of exchanging my time (a lot of it) for money, I finally reversed my negative, debt-based way of living. It was at that time I finally had something worth losing. It was then that I had to adjust my thinking and learn more about money. I did not want to lose what I had worked hard for.

So, let's go back to the original question: What is money?

Please allow me to start with the basics here. I want to reinforce what you already know or build a solid foundation of understanding upon which we can build some more complex concepts that you need to know. Fair enough?

Great. Here we go.

Money is simply a medium of exchange for one good or service for another. Usually, in a person's life, it is initially exchanged for his or her time. The time exchanged for money gives it value to the person who earned the money. Each person will have a different exchange rate based on that person's skill level or value to the employer. Another way of saying this is that each person's value to the workplace varies.

Now, the actual money itself, in today's financial world, has no meaningful value. In the United States, you can lay a $1 bill next to a $100 bill for examination. What are the differences? What makes one piece of paper more valuable than the other? Is it something precious that is woven in the paper? Hold it up to the light and see. After careful examination, you are likely to discover that the only difference is the ink design and a couple extra zeros printed behind the number one. In other countries, the bill size may vary, but it's still the same result: no real value. These notes are simply a special paper with special ink. Now hold that idea in your head. There is more.

I have a question for you now: Why do you think the $100 bill is worth more than the $1 bill? Your examination revealed that the bills are made the same, right? Have you ever heard of the term "fiat money"? Don't be shy about answering "no." I had never heard of it either. The first time I heard it, I thought I must have missed that class in high school. As I began my journey of financial discovery, the term fiat kept coming up—fiat this and fiat that. And the more I read, the more I wondered what this Italian car manufacturer had to do with anything related to the financial system. I just had no clue what was meant by this term, within this context.

So, let's define it.

Fiat money is government-issued currency that is not backed by a physical commodity, such as gold or silver, but rather by the government that issued it. The value of fiat money is derived from the relationship between supply and demand and the stability of the issuing government, rather than the worth of a commodity backing it, as is the case for "commodity money" (which we know of as gold, silver, and copper).

So, fiat money is currency that is NOT backed by something that carries physical value, but commodity money IS. This means that, with today's technology, you don't need to have the physical fiat money in your possession as you would with gold or silver. This is evident as most of us can easily see our bank account online or at an Automated Teller Machine (ATM), and it shows how many dollars are in the account. This account value is shown in the form of digits on the screen.

My version of the definition of fiat money is this: Fiat money is a **_belief_** that the money used, in most countries, has a perceived value, and the people agree to this value to use it for exchange of goods and/or services.

I want to ask you a question. If you had the ability to print a perfect replica of a U.S. dollar, euro, or peso note, could you do it legally? That, my friends, is exactly what our governments do. For us, this act would be considered counterfeiting. For the governments, it is production of legal tender. The money you work so hard for is fiat (*fake*), and its only value resides within a belief that it has value.

I consider this a great deception. How about you?

$ $

PLAIN & SIMPLE BREAKDOWN

The takeaway is that money in today's world is worthless paper with numbers printed on it that we all agree to work for and to use to buy goods and/or services. Later, I will show you why this matters, because the entities that create money do not have the necessary restraints to keep from creating more from thin air. This basic concept is our starting point to deeper knowledge. We are going to build on this concept, so keep your mind open because there is more. A lot more.

CHAPTER 2

GOLD AND SILVER AS MONEY

"A system of capitalism presumes sound money, not fiat money manipulated by a central bank. Capitalism cherishes voluntary contracts and interest rates that are determined by savings, not credit creation by a central bank."
—**Ron Paul** (1935-), U.S. Politician, Author and Physician

O ver the history of mankind, different items were used as money. Even seashells were once used as money. The most stable economy anywhere in the world has been proven with the use of gold and/or silver as money. These two metals used as money were the basis for a tried-and-true monetary system for over 4,000 years. They are solid stores of value as they exchange the time to mine for them, refine them, and mint them for use in any given economy. These metals are extremely difficult to find, and that's exactly why they are considered rare commodities. Additionally, much of the gold and silver that has been discovered and mined is still being used in one form or another, such as for bullion, coins, and jewelry. These metals are rare commodities that never disappear or vanish.

I look at any asset this way: if I can burn an asset with a match, that asset has the potential of vanishing and diminishing to zero in value.

This is not good—you don't want your asset's value to drop to zero. So, can I light a plot of land on fire? Technically, no. The items on the surface may burn, but the land will always be there. Can I light a gold coin on fire? How about a paper stock or bond from the stock market? How about a $1 bill? This is my highly technical way of determining the possibility of an asset to go to a zero value. If it can burn, look out. This concept is essentially the line of thinking behind the statement: "Gold is money, everything else is credit." That statement is attributed to JP Morgan while testifying before the US Congress in 1912, shortly before his death. If you are relying on the value of an asset that has the potential of dropping to zero value, you are essentially relying on credit.

Like the Olympic Medals, gold (awarded for 1st place) is more valuable than silver (awarded for 2nd place). Using these metals as money provides a stable financial system. Gold and silver intrinsically have value that is recognized worldwide, and the amount of gold or silver available directly correlates to what has been mined. This amount of available gold or silver is typically called "above ground." Since there is a limit placed on the money used in an economy due to availability of these metals, prices are controlled, and inflation is minimized. Unfortunately, we no longer live in a world that has a financial system that uses these metals. Soon I will reveal the reasons why this financial system is no longer in place.

As you venture into the financial world, you may hear the term "counter-party risk" as it pertains to investments. Counter-party risk simply means there is a risk that the other party in an investment, credit, or trading transaction may not fulfill his or her part of a trade or deal. In the case of gold and silver, they do not have a counter-party risk. What this means is that due to silver and gold's classification as real money, they are not dependent on someone or something else to give them value.

Most other investments do come with counter-party risks—for example, credit, trading transactions (stocks and bonds), and real estate to list a few.

> **$URPRI$E!** The Romans, during their Empiric reign, used gold and silver as money. Toward the end of the collapse of the empire, it was discovered that "coin clipping" was occurring. Coin clipping is when the coin still had the same value due to a perception that it was a particular weight (value imprinted on the coin), yet the citizens were clipping the edges of the coins and removing a very small amount of the material. After having collected enough clippings from many donor coins, a new coin could be made.

As humans do, we always try to find a better way of doing things. Improving and evolving is just in our nature. One example of this is when the United States adopted the "Gold Standard." Rather than having to haul around gold coins to pay for goods or services or having to go to the bank each time you needed something, it was determined that exchanging gold for a currency note (the U.S. dollar) provided a much easier way to pay for and sell goods and services. What the Gold Standard guaranteed is that the bank stored the gold, and the holder of a gold certificate could go to a local bank and exchange the currency back to gold, if ever desired. This new system created trust in the currency, as the note was backed by something that held actual value: gold. The Gold Standard also restricted the printing of money beyond the amount of gold available to an economy.

As a simplified example, if an economy had gold stores valued at $1 million, it would only be allowed to print $1 million worth of paper notes. That meant the exchange would be an exchange of one to one. The entire collection of currency notes would be equal to the amount of gold available. This system prevented the de-valuing of the currency and held inflation to a minimum.

$IDE NOTE: Before World War I (around 1914), one ounce of gold was equal to $20.67 in U.S. dollars. In the early 2020s, an ounce of gold was equal to $1,800-1,900 U.S. dollars.

In 1933, President Franklin D. Roosevelt changed the rule of the United States monetary system. What occurred was the first major step toward removing the U.S. dollar from the Gold Standard, and this step allowed the U.S. Government to ease the restrictions of printing money. This rule change required all citizens and banks to turn over their gold to the Federal Reserve. It also changed the policy that U.S. dollar bills were no longer used to redeem gold, and it made it illegal for anyone other than the Federal Reserve to own gold in the United States.

Ready for some devious moves? In 1934, after most of the gold had been surrendered to the U.S. Government, the Gold Reserve Act was signed into law. This act changed the value of gold to $35.00 per ounce. So, to put this into perspective, the previous gold holders (citizens and banks) were forced to surrender their gold at $20.67 per ounce, and the U.S. Government re-valued the gold for a profit of $14.33 per ounce. This was done during the Great Depression, and it makes me wonder how the American people felt about this.

Then, taking this one step further, in 1971, President Richard Nixon made a move to totally sever the tie between gold and the U.S. dollar. He did this by issuing Executive Order 11615: "Providing for Stabilization of

Prices, Rents, Wages, and Salaries." This was initially declared a temporary order on August 15th, 1971. But on October 15, 1971, President Nixon turned this into a permanent action via Executive Order 11627: "Further Providing for the Stabilization of the Economy." This order addressed several points, but for the purposes of our discussion, we'll focus on the gold and how it was severed, or decoupled, from the U.S. dollar.

$IDE NOTE: The fiat US Dollar turned 50 years old on August 15, 2021. This is the celebration of the "golden jubilee"!

The main goal of this order was to stop foreign governments that were holding the U.S. dollar from exchanging their dollars for gold payments. For the last fifty years, the U.S. dollar held the distinguished title of the World's Reserve Currency, and that meant most of the trade between countries used the U.S. dollar. This even meant the dollar was used with trades between other nations that didn't include the United States. Additionally, prior to the time this order was issued, the foreign nations that had excess U.S. currency could still trade these dollars for gold from the Federal Reserve in the United States. So, what some of these foreign governments started to do was demand gold payments instead of purchasing goods that were made in the U.S. This led to rapid dwindling of the U.S. gold reserves (gold leaving the U.S.), which caused President Nixon to act by suspending this trade via the executive order. Although the run on the U.S. gold reserves was stopped, this executive order also empowered the Federal Reserve's ability to add to the money supply without any restrictions, since the U.S. dollar was no longer coupled to gold. This is when the U.S. dollar first became fiat currency.

In 1974, President Gerald Ford revoked the executive order that President Roosevelt enacted for gold surrender and restored the ability of private ownership of gold for banks and citizens. However, this did not return the U.S. dollar to the Gold Standard.

Are you beginning to see the path that led to our current financial system? What I mean is, the original intent of money is to be a store of value, and it usually starts with trust that it is secured by something tangible like gold or silver. Over time, it becomes corrupted, and the money evolves into currency, and then the currency eventually becomes worthless.

Today, all the global money is fiat, and yet we still consider our currency as a store of value. What other choice do we have? There are many topics left to expose in this book, and we will. But for now, let me explain, in detail, how I see the global monetary system and the possibilities of it evolving into a different system. Did you notice that I did not say a "better" system?

Historically, in most sound economies, a monetary system begins with trust. Trust starts with knowing your money will serve the three functions of money: a medium of exchange, a unit of account and a store of value. The public trusts that there is value in the gold and silver coins. Gold and silver is simple to understand and cannot be counterfeited. Allow a period to pass and then an idea is sold to the public to use something else, like notes or bills, in lieu of those bulky coins, and deposit them in one place such as a bank. Once this happens, the value is transferred from the possession of the people as the bank is now the holder of the value. This is when the bank can begin to issue extra notes, as no one will know that there are more notes than gold unless there is a bank run.

$IDE NOTE: A bank run is when the people demand their deposits from any banking institution, usually due to a lack of trust in the bank. This is when the bank is exposed for not maintaining the deposits of the account holders and cannot return 100 percent of the deposits.

This is a form of manipulation of the money and marks the beginning of a fiat currency system. Are you thinking about what happens next to transition money to currency? So, another period of time elapses, and hardly anyone goes back for their gold. Instead, they continue using the currency. You may be thinking, "What can go wrong? The money is safely stored in the bank." Over time, the bankers realize that people leave their gold in the bank. They now can begin to issue extra currency, and yet the gold deposits do not increase. No one is the wiser. Then greed steps in (inherent character flaw of humans), and now it seems it is almost a challenge to see how much they can get away with by printing more and more. It is kind of like what the Romans did with the coin clipping act.

While this is happening, everyone benefits from having more currency in the system. They benefit by increased wages, which leads to affordability for more goods and services and even growth of the community. This creates a cycle that is temporary though, and it will end with a consequence. That consequence is inflation. Inflation happens when there is too much currency in the system and prices begin to increase. Once this happens, it requires more currency to be injected into the economy, and that starts a new cycle. This cycle will continue until suddenly it cannot any longer.

A rule of thumb to know is that currency always needs a place to go. The more currency in the economy, the more prices rise for goods and services. People make more currency and pay more for goods and services. The problem with inflation is when goods and services increase, but wages do not. That is when inflation becomes a real threat to people's livelihoods, as families cannot keep up with the pace (or rate) of inflation. On the other hand, inflation can slow down when more goods and services are created within an economy.

$
PLAIN & SIMPLE BREAKDOWN

What I want you to take away from this chapter is that when money is used for wages, goods, and services, it must be trusted. Gold and silver have earned that trust over time and is usually a great place to start a monetary system. However, due to the scarcity of precious metals, it limits a government's purchasing power. The desire or need for more money is and always will be a constant within society (doesn't everybody want more money?), and it justifies an economy to transition to a fiat currency system. At the time, it seems like the leaders who make this decision have found the way to prosperity. When this occurs, it will eventually lead to the destruction of that fiat currency system. This has happened every time it has been tried. Some countries last longer than others, but the end is always the same. Fiat currency always goes to its true value: zero. Remember the match analogy about burning assets? Can any nation's paper currency NOT be burned?

It all works fine until it does not. Profound saying, right? Now, we have an idea of money and currency, and you are probably thinking that this system is bigger than my local bank. So, who is behind the fake money system?

CHAPTER 3

THE FEDERAL RESERVE BANK AND CENTRAL BANKS OF THE WORLD

"Give me control of a nation's money and I care not who makes the laws."
— **Mayer Amschel Rothschild** (1744-1812),
Founder of the Rothschild Banking Dynasty
and the "Father of International Finance

These guys. Pure geniuses they are. They have mastered the art of deception. Okay, enough of my satire. Did you know that the Federal Reserve is neither federal nor is it a reserve? Or, did you know that over the past fifty years, they have provided currency to our fiat monetary system without having any tangible assets to back up the currency? In other words, this institution provides the cash but doesn't have the gold to back it up. Does this make you question why we should trust our money? Maybe not, so let me see if I can shine some light on this for you.

Oh, how the questions and tears began flowing as I peeled back the onion layers about these institutions. Let me start with a quick history lesson. In 1913, President Woodrow Wilson signed into law the Federal

Reserve Act, creating the Federal Reserve Bank. To keep this at a basic understanding level, this act was intended to supply and manage credit to the U.S. monetary system via the U.S. Treasury and the Federal Reserve Banking System. The reason there was a need for this was because there were many stability issues with previous monetary models, and the U.S. Government desired a more stable money system. So, in the Federal Reserve Bank's infancy, a global reserve currency did not exist, and the money in the United States was real. For example, during this era, precious metals were used in the coins (copper, nickel, and silver), and the paper money was redeemable for gold and silver that was stored in local banks. What was created was an honest monetary system.

As I stated earlier, the Federal Reserve Bank is not an entity of the U.S. Federal Government, nor is it run by the U.S. Federal Government. Because of the name "Federal Reserve," <u>many of us logically assume</u> it is a branch of the U.S. Government. I do not know if it was given this name with the intent to deceive, but I know I never thought otherwise.

\$IDE NOTE: In Article I, Section 10 of the US Constitution, our founders wrote: "make any Thing but gold and silver Coin a Tender in Payment of Debts;"

The Federal Reserve Bank is a privately owned company, made up of private bankers, both foreign and domestic. Take note that the only hint of control by the U.S. Government is by way of the sitting U.S. President's power to appoint the seven "governors," who make up the Board of Governors of the Federal Reserve. And, just to be clear, these people are not elected governors of different states. They are private citizens, who are appointed to the board and are called "governors." They each serve a fourteen-year term.

So, now we know that the Federal Reserve Bank (often called the "Fed") is not actually a federal agency at all. As for the second part of the name, "Reserve Bank," you guessed it. It is not a reserve bank. You cannot go to the Federal Reserve Bank for a loan or to make a deposit or a withdrawal. I will explain more about what a reserve bank is. You will be amazed with what the powers to be get away with, I promise.

Again, keeping this at intro-level knowledge, just know that reserve banks do not hold reserves of cash for you and me. Here is the fun part: the Federal Reserve does control the creation of cash (currency, that is). Recall the earlier discussion about the Gold Standard. Think of the Gold Standard as a kind of "revolutions-per-minute (RPM) governor" for an engine, which keeps the engine from revving too fast. If you were to floor the gas pedal of your car, and you had no limitation to keep it from spinning too fast, it would surely do serious damage and might even blow up the engine. That is what the Gold Standard did for the U.S. dollar. Gold kept the value of the dollar intact.

$IDE NOTE: The Federal Reserve System (FRS) is the US Central Bank and is comprised of 12 regional banks in major cities of the US. They are: New York, NY; Chicago, IL; Atlanta, GA; Minneapolis, MN; San Francisco, CA; Philadelphia, PA; Boston, MA; Cleveland, OH; Richmond, VA; Kansas City, MO; Dallas, TX; and St. Louis, MO.

For Every Act There is a Reaction

But remember the executive order that Nixon signed? With the stroke of a pen, the President of the U.S. decoupled the dollar from gold, and it was "off to the races" for the U.S. dollar. His action removed the Gold Standard—in other words, it removed the rpm limits on the US monetary system. At first, this wasn't a huge deal. When the U.S. dollar and gold initially divorced, the Fed behaved by managing currency supply to the banks and the interest rates at which they loaned the currency.

Remember, without backing currency to an asset or commodity (like gold), the currency is fiat, and it will begin to move to its true value. The Fed managed this devaluation (or descent) by the rate at which they added currency to the system and the interest rates they charged for doing so. It is a balancing act: if too much currency was added, it could create too much inflation, and if interest rates were not set correctly, it could impact economic growth negatively. All the while, the public's trust in the currency must be maintained as it truly is fake (or fiat).

The primary interest rates are called federal fund rates, and most banking interest rates in the U.S. directly correlate to the federal fund rate. Banks will pay dividends (interest) on savings accounts and make loans based on this rate. For simplicity, if they want to stimulate an economy, the rate goes down, which encourages more lending. Conversely, to slow an economy down, they raise the rates.

This control, while working with the currency supply, balanced the economy overall and gave value to the now fiat currency. But think of the consequences. If you are a saver (holding your cash deposits in a bank account), and the Fed decreases interest rates, what happens to the return on your investment in the bank? Right. The interest rate lowers, and if it goes down too much, you may want to consider a better investment because you are most likely earning very little or nothing at all. If you decide to invest your money elsewhere and go withdraw your funds from the bank, that would, in turn, draw the bank's reserves down, creating a series of other problems.

The good side is if you are not a saver but, instead, are a borrower, you have access to cheap money (low interest rates). But those low interest rates also come with consequences because it encourages people to take on more debt. Several central banks around the world have taken their fund rate to the negative territory. This situation diminishes any hope of interest rate earnings for the people who have saved currency in their local banks. Imagine those who were counting on their savings account interest earnings to supplement their incomes as part of their retirement plans.

So, as you can see, there must be a balancing act to keep the U.S. dollar in its world reserve currency status.

Now you know that our currency is fake, or in other words, fiat. You also know that the U.S. dollar is the world reserve currency, and all other country's currencies have coupled their individual value to the U.S. dollar. The global economies are all interconnected. To think we can somehow isolate ourselves from what our neighbors across the world are experiencing is pure fantasy. You also know that currency can be created without any limits if the Elites decide the conditions warrant this act.

And if you have been paying attention, in the year 2020, the world entered a crisis so massive, we've never seen anything like it before. What was the initial response to this global crisis? Yes, to print more currency. A lot more. Trillions of dollars were created. Looking back, the Fed and the US Treasury created over 40% of all US Dollars during this time. Before entering the global pandemic, we were already in the red zone – that indicator on your control panel that alerts you when your engine running too hot. I cannot emphasize enough how dangerous that situation can be. Let's see what this is going to cost us. Should we expect a period of high inflation?

We are up to speed now with what the Fed is and how they operate. But it does not stop there. There is a world banking system, and most countries have a central bank. Within the world banking system, the Fed is the top central bank, and controls the world reserve currency. Just imagine that the central banks operate the same way as the Fed except they do not control the U.S. dollar. They only control the currency for the given country they are in.

Due to this structure, countries can manage their own fiat currency and if mismanaged, the currency can quickly go to zero value. If managed well, the currency will devalue at a much slower rate. The rule for fiat currency is all fiat goes to its true value: zero. How quickly it gets there is the role of the central banks. What you should look out for is inflation. Over the past hundred years of different fiat systems, inflation will rise slowly, almost unnoticeably, and then suddenly the economy collapses.

Let me introduce a few of the recent events to illustrate this. We have the German Weimar Republic, Republic of Zimbabwe, Argentina, and Venezuela to name a few. Then, in 2020-2021, the world experienced a pandemic that tried to keep people at home and paid them to do so. The limits that kept economies in check were raised (or removed). Governments went deeper and deeper in debt and spent more and more.

Regardless of the nobility of the reasons, it is still debt from printing trillions of U.S. dollars or other central bank's fiat. Keeping the economy afloat is a monumental and expensive task, but somehow, the creators of cash — the central banks of the world, seem to be able to just authorize creation of currency without any assets to back it and POOF—magically, currency is created. This scenario is a lot more complex than that, but that is a simple explanation of what is happening.

Another way they create currency is through the banking system. Banks in the U.S. that are part of the Federal Reserve System have the ability to create money as well.

Wait, what? My local branch bank can create money? How is that?

Check this out. Here is the unbelievable stuff I mentioned earlier…

Let's say you want to buy a car, a house, or something that requires a loan. When the bank approves the loan, they create the digits in the computer and pay the seller for the good(s) you are borrowing the currency for. Until recently, bank lending used to be called fractional banking. Fractional banking required the bank to hold a tenth of what was loaned. This was their reserve, and the rest of the money was created. Then, that cash that was just created normally went to another account of the seller. That currency would be used for more lending and creation for the receiving bank. This would go on and on.

To illustrate this, let's look at a simple example. Sally wants to buy a house and needs $100,000 from the bank, so she will need a loan. Under a fractional banking system, the bank would be required to have ten percent of the loan amount, or $10,000, in reserves in order to approve this loan for Sally. When Sally is approved for the loan, the bank gives the seller $100,000. As long as the bank holds $10,000 in reserves, they can create (out of thin air) $100,000 to lend. Sally will make her loan payments, with interest, to the bank that created the currency. Now, the seller would normally deposit this newly created currency in their bank. This deposit is now available to create $1 million in new loans. They can do this as they now have the required ten percent for reserves. This is fractional reserve banking. This cycle continues over and over and over and creates liquidity in the economy. When this slows or stops, then a liquidity crisis occurs.

In 2020, due to the fragile economy, the fractional reserve part was removed, meaning the tenth was no longer required to be held back by the lender. The bank created currency out of thin air and lent it to you with interest. So, using our example, that means to loan Sally the $100,000 for her house, the bank isn't required to have ANY funds in reserve at all. Can you believe this? Why should a bank get to create currency and loan it to you, all to make more currency? Doesn't it feel like the banks are cheating—making currency on borrowed currency they never even had in the first place?

If your head is swimming with more questions than answers at this point, don't worry. You're not alone. Researching and learning about the Federal Reserve and central banks—and the system created for them and by them—is a complex process for a reason. The institutions do not want people like you and me (the masses) to know about the gig they have going. However, because you picked up this book, I know you want to have a better understanding of how to manage your currency and thrive in today's monetary system. That means you need to dig a bit deeper under the surface of some of these more complex topics.

For a simple understanding of the system, try to divide the banking system into smaller pieces. For example, the way I look at it is there are two types of spenders in an economy: government and private. Okay, now, government spending, in today's world, is usually done with debt, as most governments spend more than they tax their citizens. That debt is issued by the country's central bank. The idea is that the loans made to governments will be repaid in full, but over the last few decades, it seems that the tax revenue generated is barely enough to service the interest accrued on any nation's debt. And without sufficient tax revenue, governments do not have sufficient funds to repay the loans to the central bank. A nation's solvency can quickly turn due to becoming insolvent due to extreme debts and then the fund lending rate is increased by the central bank to combat inflation, for example. Simply put, the larger the debt, the larger the debt service payments. Then the cycle starts over and repeats. In the private sector, the currency is loaned to a person or company and is repaid with interest by the recipient of the loan. Can you imagine operating a business or household the way a government does? You would most likely fail. This is your introduction to Keynesian economics (don't worry, we'll get into this in a later chapter).

I encourage all to have a deeper understanding of our banking system. I am certain that most people are not alright with banks enriching themselves in a game they created for us, and the more knowledge we have, the better we are at protecting ourselves within this game. I will continue to peel back additional layers as we journey further into the book. For now, I will wrap up this discussion with my take on this whole scam—er… I mean system.

$
PLAIN & SIMPLE BREAKDOWN

The main takeaway from this chapter is that our currency is regulated by a private company, not a federal agency. This private entity is legally allowed to create currency out of thin air, ever since the dollar was decoupled from gold. *All* currency is loaned into existence and must be paid back with interest. Therefore, the debt could never be repaid in its entirety, as there will never be enough currency in existence due to the interest associated with the loans. In summary, the Federal Reserve Bank is a central bank, and all central banks are companies that create their own currency and loan it to governments, businesses, and citizens. Then the governments, businesses, and citizens are required to pay the loans back with currency the central banks created... plus interest. What an awesome deal... for the bank.

Now, all of this currency creation and lending created this thing called a debt trap. This can go on for a very long time, but eventually it will come to an end, and what we are witnessing now are the end stages of this system. The end is a collapse of the monetary system as we know it. Remember, all fiat will go to its real value of zero. In the U.S., loan interest rates went to historical lows. Internationally, central banks were lending their fiat at negative interest rates. Imagine collecting negative one percent in interest on your savings account. Yes, you figured it correctly: you will pay the bank to hold your deposits. Remember, low interest rates are rolled out to stimulate an economy and create liquidity. What is happening and what I want you to see is this: The central banks know that they cannot leave interest rates as low as they are because they are inducing more bad debt and bad behavior (as it relates to borrowing). However, they also know they cannot raise the interest rates to the level needed to control inflation because then they would trigger the very crisis, or collapse, they are trying to avoid. There is no way out, other than to keep doing what they are doing, but by doing that, they are making it worse. The global economy is massive, and it would require a series of events to create a monetary crisis. By late spring of 2022, the Federal Reserve began tightening the money supply by raising the federal funds rate. At the end of 2022, the small rate hikes have already slowed the US housing and auto market drastically. This is only the beginning as inflation is topping 40-year highs. The world has never had a universally-accepted global reserve currency that was fiat. So, what can **we** do? All we can do is educate, watch, and create possibilities for the future, because there are no certainties in a situation that has never been experienced before. That is the caveat to a potential global collapse. As I predicted, 2023 started off with a looming global recession and high inflation. Never forget that the institutions and governments that created this mess are the ones we are relying on to get us out of it. Does this make you feel secure with the institutions and countries' monetary policies? The majority of countries' currencies are tied to the reserve currency of the U.S. dollar. Let's dive further into this topic.

CHAPTER 4

WORLD RESERVE CURRENCY

"I am absolutely convinced that no wealth in the world can help humanity forward, even in the hands of the most devoted worker in this cause. The example of great and pure characters is the only thing that can produce fine ideas and noble deeds. Money only appeals to selfishness and always tempts its owners irresistibly to abuse it."
—**Albert Einstein** (1879-1955), Theoretical Physicist

The world has become smaller. Have you ever heard that? What does that mean to you? Is it because of modern day transportation methods like planes that can take us to all the corners of the globe in a matter of hours? Is it perhaps because of the internet, a marvel that connects us with billions of people in just a few clicks? Maybe it is because of our economies and how most countries can trade and play nice with each other.

This is another complex topic (do you notice a theme of complexity yet?), and I am going to share with you my simple version. Many people in the U.S. do not realize how the dollar they use is also used to connect nations. Also, many people outside of the U.S. do not know how connected their currency is to the U.S. dollar.

Here is a quick history lesson. In 1944, after World War II, developed nations of the world got together to work out a new global monetary system. The intent was to govern monetary relations among independent states. This is when the Bretton Woods Agreement was negotiated by delegates of 44 different countries. Global monetary policy was agreed upon by all, and one of the results was the recognition of the U.S. dollar as the world reserve currency. The delegates favored the U.S., as the U.S. had two-thirds of the world's gold in storage, and the U.S. dollar was backed by gold already.

$IDE NOTE: Bretton Woods is the name of the town in New Hampshire where this meeting took place.

From this point, the U.S. dollar was backed by gold and all other currencies valued their own currency in comparison to the U.S. dollar. Remember, the U.S. dollar was backed by gold all the way up until 1971 when the divorce of the U.S. dollar from gold happened.

Since that point, the U.S. dollar is no longer limited by gold. Why am I sharing this with you? How does this affect the average citizen? Well, I am glad you asked. For the American citizen, using a currency that is identified as the world reserve currency is great. The Federal Reserve Bank and the U.S. Government are now in control of the money supply. Due to the U.S. dollar being used around the world for trading, it was in high demand, per the Bretton Woods Agreement. As economies grew over time, this also meant that more money was needed to do business and trade abroad. Remember, all countries had their currency pegged (valued) in comparison to the U.S. dollar to stabilize their own economies, while the U.S. dollar was valued in comparison to gold.

That was a good benefit—for a while. Remember, the United States was immensely powerful and stable after World War II, so, the stability of the U.S. dollar was more important than any other nation's currency, as all other currencies used the U.S. dollar to give their own currency value. The system we all live in is attached to the fate of the stewardship of the U.S. dollar.

Let's jump back to 1971, because that year was a major turning point for economies around the world. We have already discussed that Richard Nixon was the U.S. president during this era, and the Vietnam War was nearing its end. Wars are awfully expensive for governments. Remember the earlier discussion on gold certificates (U.S. dollars) and how people could take their certificates to the bank and exchange them for gold on demand? For U.S. citizens, they could do this up until 1933, that is. Well, since the U.S. had issued so many dollars abroad for trading between countries, some had built up a surplus of dollars and were exchanging their supply for U.S. gold.

The British attempted a $750 million exchange for gold, and President Nixon was advised that giving up the U.S. gold was not sustainable. The quickest way to stop this was for the U.S. to decouple the gold from the dollar. This move was temporary, for a period of only ninety days. President Nixon did this through an executive order that has been amended twice since then to extend it, and it has never been rescinded to this day.

Internet Fun Search: Google "Executive Order 11627 of October 15, 1971; Further Providing for the Stabilization of the Economy" to read the exact language of the order.

As you can see from the title of the executive order, "Further Providing for the Stabilization of the Economy," President Nixon was attempting to deal with an economic downturn in 1971 with wage, salary, and rent controls to keep inflation in check at that time. As a side effect of the removal of the Gold Standard, politicians discovered the term "free money," or fiat currency. In the beginning, it appeared that our politicians were responsible stewards of the U.S. dollar. After all, they were responsible to forty-four other nations that depended on the U.S. to be good stewards.

Remember, all currencies were being loaned into existence, because they had been transformed to fiat currency. Without a connection to a tangible asset like gold, there were no restrictions to how much currency could be printed. As U.S. Presidents came and went over the next 50 years, the U.S. debt reached more than $27 trillion dollars. Moreover, by the end of 2022, the US government debt rapidly approached $31.5 trillion.

What is ironic about the whole situation is that during the 2012 and 2016 presidential elections, candidates brought up this debt topic in their campaigns. They said things like, "You are spending your children's money and your children's children's money." I do not recall anyone talking like this during the most recent presidential election in 2020. I think everyone has figured out that this debt will never be repaid, so let's not speak of the elephant in the room that is the U.S. debt.

The United States of America has enemies. Two come to mind have become extremely powerful economically and militarily, and we will talk about them shortly. First, I want you to try to imagine the pride of a powerful nation being forced to trade with other countries using your enemy's currency. What do you think they want to do? My thought is that they would like to take control of the world reserve currency.

$IDE NOTE: There are two golden rules I know of. The first is explained by Jesus: "Therefore, whatever you want men to do to you, do also to them, for this is the Law and the Prophets." Matthew 7:12. The secular version that applies in this case is, "He who has the gold, makes the rules."

Wealth is power, and, unfortunately, he who controls the money controls the world. Unfortunately, we still live in a world that has people who seek dominion overall. And currently, there are the two countries that can now rival the United States. Oh, who do I think they are? If you guessed them to be the Russian Federation and the People's Republic of China, you would be correct. Both countries have been seeking ways to trade with other nations without the use of the U.S. dollar. Additionally, they have been really focused on procuring and stockpiling gold for many years now and establishing their own currency that would be backed by their own gold. The strategy in this would be to use currency that is backed by an asset, whereas the U.S. dollar is fiat. It would be attractive for nations to have a stable currency backing their own.

$IDE NOTE:: If you ever go to China with any gold, you better declare it upon entry, or you more than likely will not be leaving with it.

The world has been led to see the U.S. as the richest nation in the world. I beg to differ. The U.S. is the most indebted nation in the world.

$ $

PLAIN & SIMPLE BREAKDOWN

Perception of wealth plays a key role to be viewed as power. It has been enabled by the freedom of the press, the currency printing press that is. When there is no restraint to the currency creation, well, it just gets out of control. Then the pressure from the public is on the politicians because they started the cycle of free or easy currency. Then it becomes next to impossible to close that door. It is like having a bag of delicious chocolate chip cookies, and you just want one. It was so delicious, you get another. Yum, that was good, why not one more? Before you know it, you ate the whole bag. Yes, we are there. I believe the U.S. dollar is out of control. We are witnessing the era of everything free. Free housing, free healthcare, free education, free food… where will it end? The world is waking up to the low cost of fiat currency, and everyone wants some. I wonder how much longer this can last. Don't you?

CHAPTER 5

PETRODOLLAR

"As long as we issue fiat currency,
I see no alternative to a legal tender law."
—**Alan Greenspan** (1926-), American Economist,
13th Chair of the Federal Reserve

W hy should I introduce you to something called the "petrodollar" when this is a plain-and-simple book about money? While I
can't argue that the petrodollar is a plain or simple topic, it is an excellent
illustration that helps to reinforce the fragility of the current monetary system. This is a global economy, and most nations are dependent upon one
another. I want you to understand that if one nation stumbles economically, the ripple effect could reach your front door.

Recall that the U.S. dollar had value when it was backed by gold
(the early years). The U.S. dollar then became the world reserve currency
(the middle years), and then it became a fiat currency (the current years).
Now, the bankers knew there had to be an element to keep the U.S. dollar relevant in the world to maintain its status. This leads to the story of
the petrodollar.

When I first heard of the petrodollar, I immediately related it to fuel and
oil plus currency. When I lived in Germany, the gas stations used the term

"petrol." A quick deduction led me to guess petro was short for petroleum, a substance found in fuel products (gasoline, oil, kerosene, etc.). Now, you may be asking, what does petro (fuel/oil) have to do with money?

In 1945, the United States and Saudi Arabia agreed to set oil prices in U.S. dollars. That meant any nation that wished to purchase oil from the kingdom of Saudi Arabia had to exchange their currency into U.S. dollars first to complete the transaction. Due to this arrangement, OPEC (Organization of the Petroleum Exporting Countries) also sold their oil in U.S. dollars. Can you imagine how it was for the enemies of the United States, having to buy U.S. dollars to purchase oil for their own countries?

Let us use a tiny bit of brainpower for a minute. Think about the U.S. dollar, and remember it was backed by gold until 1971. Also, all nations that were part of the central banking system used the U.S. dollar to back their own currency. Through this coupling to the U.S. dollar, their fiat money had value. Now, add the petrodollar to the mix.

I believe the petrodollar system is really the only reason the U.S. dollar has been able to maintain its status as the world reserve currency after Nixon removed it from the Gold Standard.

And have you ever noticed how involved the United States military has been in the Middle East for so many decades? I served in the U.S. Air Force for twenty-two years and spent many months in various places in the Middle East. Whenever a conflict or war reared its ugly head, people said, "It's about the oil." I toed that line too—back then. Now I see it a different way: The U.S. was protecting the petrodollar system. That was the true reason—the mighty U.S. dollar. It was too important to risk the world reserve status shifting to any other nation.

Remember the golden rule about controlling the money? Let's be honest, the U.S. does not want to relinquish its power, and in today's economy, control of money is power. The Middle Eastern OPEC nations also benefitted by way of the protection of the U.S. military. If you look at history, that era is around the time the United States' military interest in the region started.

I also noticed how the People's Republic of China, the Russian Federation and the Islamic Republic of Iran are all rising in economic strength. What do they have in common? They share a desire to end the petrodollar system. These large economies are weening themselves off U.S. dollar dependency. They are doing this by trading goods (oil from Iran) with each other and using their own currency or gold to conduct the exchanges.

$ $

PLAIN & SIMPLE BREAKDOWN

The key take away about the petrodollar system is that the United States needs this system to stay in place to protect the U.S. dollar's world reserve status. The dollar maintains its relevancy by forcing all nations that are dependent upon oil imports to purchase oil with the U.S. dollar. Some countries are trying to replace this system with their own currency and, in turn, desire to become the world's new reserve currency.

Here is a quick breakdown: The U.S. dollar depends on oil to have value, all currencies in the central banking system depend on the U.S. dollar to have value, and if the demand for oil decreases dramatically, it will affect the value of the U.S. dollar. Can you see the global connection? Can you see the fragility of the monetary system in this instance?

CHAPTER 6

TAXES

"There can be no such thing as 'fairness in taxation.' Taxation is nothing but organized theft, and the concept of a 'fair tax' is therefore every bit as absurd as that of 'fair theft.'"
—**Murray Rothbard** (1926-1995),
American Economist and Historian, Political Theorist

Virtually everyone in the U.S., citizens and visitors, will pay some type of tax if they spend any money. This is true in many other countries as well.

$IDE NOTE: I recall when living in Germany that the sales taxes were extremely high. But if you had a larger purchase, you could apply for a VAT (Value Added Tax) refund upon departing the country. I am quite sure that is not available in the United States.

What is the reason for taxes? Well, most of us understand that paying taxes is a way of collecting from the public to fund various services needed in a society. Property taxes, for example, pay for schools, roads, and police. Fuel tax is used to cover driving-related spending. Personal Income Tax (federal) was permanently enacted in 1913 by the Sixteenth

Amendment to the U.S. Constitution and was primarily used to pay for war debts. Overall, the average U.S. resident is liable for up to 97 different taxes. You must ask yourself why? What is it like in other countries?

If you really get your head in the game and dig into your spending, you are most likely to find that taxes are at the top of your list for your biggest expenses. Where does it all go? I remember when I had my first job and was making $3.35 per hour. I calculated my wages by multiplying the hours worked. I came up with a number around $90-$100 in one week. I worked as a gas station attendant at an Amoco gas station after school in Reston, Virginia.

When I got my first paycheck, I was so disappointed to see that it was in the low $60 dollar range. I think everyone learns this lesson from their first paycheck. After that initial shock, you learn to accept this and think, *I must work more if I want more.* At least that is how I thought. Heck, it was taken from you before you even touched it. What could you do?

Then, after you finally find that job that pays well, you discover that even more money is taken from your paycheck. Now you must do something. You realize that you are the same person who paid $30 or so in taxes at one point, and now you may be paying $1,000, $10,000, or even more. And that is just one person's taxes. And just income tax. What about the ninety-six other types of taxes being paid by 330 million or so people? The numbers really add up, and now you need to look for ways to start keeping some of that cash that you have earned. The U.S. Government seems like it is one hungry, fiery furnace, and it will take whatever you give it and just burn it up somehow.

The question for me is, why are there so many taxes? Why are the taxes so much? I have said and heard others say that we want to pay our fair share. But what is fair? All a person *should* be taxed for are the things common to each person in the country they live in. Examples of these things are roads, defense or policing, and minimum government services. That is not the case though, is it?

Were you taught about the tax laws of your country and how to reduce your liability in paying some of them? Did you even think it was possible to take actions to relieve your tax burdens? The answer is more than likely no. I certainly wasn't. Why not, then? How would you ever find out about any actions you could take to reduce your liability to your taxes?

In the U.S., I observe wealthy people pay little, or even nothing, compared to the person working hard at an average-paying job. The people of the working class are the ones who bear the burden of taxation. I want you to know, though, that it does not have to be this way. Remember the second Golden Rule: "He who has the gold makes the rules." The wealthy (the gold owners) have written the tax laws to minimize their taxation. This is done through lobbyists and the lawmakers. You too can learn the laws they have written for themselves and use them to your advantage. But no one told you this little detail, did they?

So, back to my question, what do you think is fair?

What if I told you that taxes are merely a tool to help prop up the government money system?

Huh? "What you talkin' 'bout Willis?"

$IDE NOTE: Willis is a character from the popular American television sitcom *Diff'rent Strokes*. This was one of the catch phrases from the show.

We'll use the U.S. dollar for this example, but you should be able to apply this concept to any central bank monetary system. We now know that the U.S. dollar is currently fiat currency. Let us say you want to work for real money, such as silver or gold, and you pay for everything with these metals. Everything works just fine until it is time to pay your taxes. Taxes must be paid in the legal tender, which is the U.S. dollar. Gotcha. You will have to exchange the silver or gold to the currency to pay any taxes. What does the US Constitution say? Hmmm, that is weird, isn't it?

Because of its standing as legal tender, and the fact that the government will accept nothing else as your tax payment, citizens share the belief that the dollar has some sort of validity or value. If you choose not to pay your taxes, just wait and see what happens. This can lead to imprisonment or seizure of your possessions, like your house, for example.

Now, if you are really thinking about the things introduced to you earlier in this book, you may have come up with the idea that if fiat is free, then why can't the U.S. Government just print the money instead of taxing the people? Well, as the holder of the world reserve currency, they could… for a little while. And that is what you see has happened during the global pandemic that emerged in 2020. They printed by the trillions. If you really dig into the numbers and what the Federal Reserve and central banks have done, they indirectly bought assets with currency that they created. I think this creates another problem for us now. Can you guess what that may be?

Our monetary system appears to have become unbridled. Have you ever known anyone who was filing bankruptcy? Imagine this person needed to file bankruptcy, because of being irresponsible with credit. The heavily indebted person's plan was to run up more debt with no intention of paying it back. From the beginning, that person planned to run up the debt and then file bankruptcy to get out of paying it back. Knowing full well that the person was about to lose the credit status previously achieved, that person decided to maximize debt. Why not, since there was no longer anything to lose? Does this scenario sound familiar on a global scale? Hmmm.

$
PLAIN & SIMPLE BREAKDOWN

This chapter's takeaway regarding taxation is that taxes, in any form (property, income, or sales, to name a few), are necessary to help give value to a nation's fiat currency. One cannot pay taxes in Mexico with U.S. dollars, and one cannot pay taxes in Japan with euros. Taxes provide added support to assist giving value to fiat. It is part of the monetary system. The way I see it, if currency is not real, then why does anyone need to pay taxes? I realize this is going to an extreme, but why do we? Central banks only need to print more money. So, why won't they do this?

Well, it's simple: If money just fell from the sky, and no one was required to pay taxes, there would be no belief that the dollar has any value. I want to stress that fiat equals belief. Without belief, the entire system falls apart.

END OF CHAPTER BONUS

In the U.S., if you ever hear a politician say, "We're gonna make the rich pay for this." as a campaign promise, beware. This is a trap, and I cannot say with certainty if it is from a place of ignorance or deceptiveness of the politician in question, but just know that the wealthy have already figured out a way to not get taxed at all.

Remember the secular golden rule described in the previous chapter? The wealthy write the rules. One major strategy I learned from the wealthy is to own nothing and control everything. They do this by creating trusts. And yes, you can too. Going back to the politician's campaign promises, it sounds good to get the wealthy to pay, but, when it is time to pay, it's typically us paying, as we did not have tax planning knowledge. Reference the 97 or more different taxes we are liable for.

CHAPTER 7

GOLD AND SILVER VALUATION

"Commodities such as gold and silver have a world market that transcends national borders, politics, religions, and race. A person may not like someone else's religion, but he'll accept his gold."
— **Robert Kiyosaki** (1947-)
Author of *Rich Dad, Poor Dad* series, Businessman

W hat is the value of gold? What is the value of silver? How is value determined for these things they call precious metals? Hmmm, those are good questions. Most people never give it much thought. They don't even think they can own precious metals in forms other than jewelry.

As a refresher, let's review: Gold and silver are real money, and they are considered a *store of value*. That store of value came from the mining process, the purification process, and the minting process. There is labor involved to create that silver bar or gold coin, or vice versa. The metal is rare and cannot be counterfeited. So what does it cost?

Here is the plain and simple answer: gold and silver values never change. Never. You may be thinking to yourself, *Here you go again, Steve, with these crazy ideas.* Well, it is true. I had a hard time thinking about their values until I got my brain wrapped around this revelation. First, we'll focus on gold and its primary function being money, or a store of value.

In 1933, when gold was deemed illegal in the U.S., it was valued by the U.S. Government to be $35 per troy ounce.

$IDE NOTE: A troy ounce is a unit of measure for weighing precious metals, dating back to the Middle Ages. One troy ounce is 31.10 grams.

This price controlled the value of the dollar. Did you catch that? The value of the dollar. The gold value does not change — it is the standard. That is where the term Gold Standard came from. Now, this standard held steady until the President Nixon era. Remember the Stabilization of the Economy Act of 1971? A couple of years later, gold was permitted to be traded on the open market. On February 27, 1973, one troy ounce was equal to $83.70. Fast forward 49 years later to November 2022, when one troy ounce of gold was $1,800 in value.

As of this writing, there is a difference of $1,765 between today's gold and what the U.S. government determined a troy ounce of gold to be in 1933. One must ask what changed? If the gold itself did not change, and the process of mining, purifying, and minting the gold did not change, then the only real possible answer is that the unit against which gold is measured changed. In this case, that is the U.S. dollar.

Does that mean the U.S. dollar is more valuable or less valuable? Of course, it is less... this is evident, as it will take more dollars to purchase the same troy ounce of gold. That means the value of the dollar is declining. And the point being made here is that this is due to the design of fiat currency. It historically goes to zero. Allow me to remind you that human beings are corruptible, and this is reflected in our monetary system.

Unlike gold, silver has two functions: It is monetary, and it is industrial. Often silver is called the "poor man's gold," because it is significantly less expensive than gold. The price of silver is often expressed in a ratio of how many silver ounces it takes to purchase one ounce of gold. Right now, that ratio is around 75 to 1. It is abnormally high due to the ETF (exchange traded funds) trading that will be explained momentarily. The normal ratio is closer to 40 to 1, and this has not been seen since around 2011. More importantly, the mining/production ratio is closer to 8 to 1! The second function is silver's industrial use in most circuitry found in computers, cell phones, and even cruise missiles.

$IDE NOTE: It takes about 50 pounds of silver to make one cruise missile. If you think of the purpose of the missile, that silver will more than likely never be reclaimed to be recycled.

Now, if I didn't muddy the waters for you with this explanation, I want to add to the mix my views of the manipulation of the gold and silver pricing on the stock market. Manipulation? No way. That is impossible. We have governments that have written laws to protect us from these evil rich people and bankers, don't we? You decide. You do not need to be a trader to understand my "Spence-ism" regarding this. Let's stay true to the promise of this book plain and simple?

Gold and silver are traded on the market, but the trades are in paper only and not the actual metal itself. That was confusing to me when I learned of this. To be honest with you, I never gave any thought to how metals were traded. Well, the markets converted the metals to paper stocks, and the metal is stored somewhere safe. The paper is exchanged (or traded), and that is how the price is determined in the market and to the physical metals.

Well, kind of…

What is typically traded on the market is called ETFs (exchange traded funds). That stands for "exchange traded futures." Futures are gold and silver to be mined in the future. Here is where you should say again, "Wait, what?" Yes, these gamblers—er…, I mean traders, trade with gold and silver that has not been mined yet. You might think that is not so bad if they know how much gold and silver are mined annually, and one can purchase the metals at a pre-determined price today for receiving it in the future.

Plain and simple, the use of the ETFs for precious metals is a tool to manipulate the physical prices of the metals. The big banks use their power to create supply and demand of gold and silver that has historically suppressed their true value.

$IDE NOTE: Here are the stats. On average, 2,500 tons of gold are mined per year, which equals 80,000,000 ounces. One gold contract ETF is equal to 100 ounces, and there are many contracts available. If you apply the supply-and-demand rule, the gold and silver physical (already mined) is tied to the ETF price which means there is more supply than demand. Also note that the supply is inflated, so the price of the physical metal results in a suppression. Many investors claim that ETFs are manipulating the true price (called discovery) of these metals. In layman's terms, a true discovery of value of the physical (real metals) cannot be determined due to the amount of ETFs (fake) created. The creation of ETFs keeps the price of physical gold and silver from finding their true value.

What is the supposed real value of gold and silver? By going to www.usdebtclock.org, you can easily look this up in real time. If you look at the far right-hand column, you will see the true exchange rate. A formula is applied and calculated in the U.S. by taking the M2 money supply and dividing it by the yearly world production of gold or silver in ounces.

$IDE NOTE: The Federal Reserve defines the M2 money supply as a measure of the money supply that includes cash and checking deposits.

Look at what is happening to the U.S. dollar right now according to the US Debt Clock website: In 1913, the dollar to silver ratio was $2.66 per ounce, and as of December 2022 it is $425 per ounce. In 1913, the dollar to gold ratio was $28.49 per ounce, compared to December 2022, which was $3,130 per ounce. This illustration shows the year over year increase amount of dollars in the US M2 money supply divided by the yearly world production of Gold or Silver (in ounces). The rate of dollar creation far exceeds the rate of gold or silver production. So, a simple deduction should be made then that the more the M2 supply (basically the amount of money pumped into the economy), the more the true value of the metals should be in an un-manipulated market. Now, compare these valuations of where they should be to where they are today (December 2022) in the market. Gold is priced about $1,800 per ounce (not $3,130), and silver is priced about $24.00 per ounce (not $425). The prices are clearly suppressed by the use of ETFs. However, this suppression, in my opinion, shows that they are on sale. They are more affordable to us, the working-class people, yet very few of us take advantage of these discounts.

Another example of gold's value, although rather crude, is the "suit" example. Essentially, since the 1800s, a person could purchase a decent man's suit with one ounce of gold and still have money left over to buy shoes, a tie, a belt, and other accessories. This is true even today: at $1,825 in U.S. dollars, a decent man's suit can be purchased with the same ounce of gold.

At this point, you may be thinking, *Wow, Steve, this is all really interesting, but why do I really need to know about the value of gold and silver?* That's a great question. My intent is to open your eyes to the monetary system we are all in and how today's currency is essentially fake (for lack of a better word) and will more than likely fail us. I don't want you to be taken by surprise.

I also want you to see what is real. There is hope for all of us, and I want to let you know that you are not doomed. Having gold and silver, to me, is not an investment, but an insurance policy due to the characteristics of their properties. They are the best store of value in the world. Simply put, consider this a revelation to provide you with a potential path to survival in the case of an economic downturn, or even worse, a collapse.

$URPRI$E! Up until the 1960s, for many countries, precious metals were used in a nation's coin system. In the U.S., ten cents (dime), twenty-five cents (quarter), fifty cents (half dollar), and the one dollar (silver dollar) coins were made up of ninety percent silver until 1964. Another fun fact is that it takes approximately $1.40 face value of these pre-1965 coins in any combination to make one ounce. Think about it: $1.40 in 1964 equals $25.50 today. Check those change jars.

$ $

PLAIN & SIMPLE BREAKDOWN

What I want you to take away from this chapter about gold and silver is that these precious metals do not ever change in value; they are the standards of value. When the price per ounce goes up or down, it is indicating the fiat currency's strength or weakness in purchasing power. Investors understand this, and most will hold the metals as an insurance policy to hedge against inflation or the normal devaluation of the fiat currency.

CHAPTER 8

GOING DIGITAL

"The black market was a way of getting around government controls. It was a way of enabling the free market to work. It was a way of opening up, enabling people."
— **Milton Friedman** (1912-2006), American Economist and Statistician, Nobel Prize Recipient in Economic Sciences

At the time of this writing, it is December 2022. I 'time stamp' this chapter as the digital space is a rapidly evolving arena and is certain to change. Now, some people have heard of digital currency, and, of course, some have not. This is, again, a simplified version of what it is. The funny thing is, most of us who spend and earn money have, in a roundabout way, already gone digital and have not even noticed.

You may ask, "How is that?" In the U.S. and, I suspect, in many other central bank countries, most people are on a direct deposit for their wages. In other words, the employer deposits their funds directly into each person's bank account. From that account, the person may have some liabilities to pay for, such as groceries, rent or a mortgage, utilities, car payments, or credit card bills. This is simply transferred from the deposited bank account to the creditor by use of an online banking platform, a debit card, or a check. In this fashion, physical cash is never used. I remember using my debit card at the gas pump for the first time. I have to say, I was very apprehensive to do that. I think I was one of the last few in my era to use this extremely easy way to pay at the pump system. Look at us now: I consider walking into a gas station a major inconvenience.

Over time as I traveled the world, I felt confident that I needed to carry less and less cash with me. The wealthier folks who traveled always had planned and traveled with travelers checks (anyone remember those?).

It really was not that long ago. Now I believe those checks are obsolete. So much has been revolutionized due to digital currency. I can use my debit card in many countries, both for direct payments and to withdraw cash in that country's local currency. I can use my card to pay for dinner or buy groceries. It is quite a benefit to be able to do these things without worrying about cash.

The conveniences of going digital will benefit our day-to-day lives, as more and more people are comfortable without having to carry cash. I have concluded for myself that we should not have a cashless society, but I constantly live a cashless life. That sentence is oxymoronic. The fact that I operate as a cashless person, I challenge myself all the time on my belief of a cash versus cashless monetary system. If I did not know anything else, I would easily side with the cashless side. Let us see where you land after a little discovery.

We have started off by explaining digital currency, and most of us in the world are already using it. Let us go one step further and describe decentralized digital currency, also known as cryptocurrency.

Wait, what?

Yes, this currency is decentralized because the transactions we described earlier used centralized currency such as the U.S. dollar, euro, peso, real, etc. All of it is currency from your central bank or Federal

Reserve that we described earlier in this book. Then what is decentralized currency? Any currency that is outside of the centralized banking system, created by the people, and purely digital.

There are three primary digital currencies currently available. They are Bitcoin, Litecoin, and Ethereum. From these primary coins, there is a sub-coin market. These are called altcoins, and there are hundreds of different types of them to select from. And then there are stable coins. These coins are commodity based and are designed to provide a crypto place to park your digital currencies without the volatility of the digital coin market. As of now, the US dollar is the commodity for most of these. Kind of funny to link up something that is called 'stable' to something that is 'fiat', isn't it? There are projects in work that would use real money such as gold and silver as the commodity. They are very close to making these coins available to the market.

Usually, to get in the digital market, one would have to purchase a primary coin with fiat currency. Cryptocurrency is normally purchased through an exchange. There are many exchanges available and note that they all do not offer the same coins. Once a purchase is made, there are one of two choices now to make. The first choice is to stop there and just own the primary coin. The second choice would be to exchange the primary coin for an altcoin. Some prefer altcoins, as they give the opportunity to buy in low (as low as a fraction of one cent) and have the chance for it to explode into prosperity. To purchase one Bitcoin, it could cost up to $18,000, as of January 2023. So, that sums the crypto coins up in a neat little package. This is a quick overview of purchasing the digital currency today. The digital space is gaining popularity by the day, and due to this popularity, it has become very volatile.

$IDE NOTE: An attractive side to owning cryptocurrency is that you can purchase any amount you wish! If you want to buy one dollar's worth, you can. If you want to buy one billion dollar's worth, you can do that too! All cryptocurrency is fractional and does not require full coin purchasing. You do not have to be a wealthy investor to purchase cryptocurrency!

Warning! If you plan to purchase altcoins, please know two things. First, there are hundreds of different kinds of altcoins, and they all have different purposes. Second, some of the altcoins are designed to simply take your money. You may hear the term "pump n dump" as it relates to meaningless altcoins. I highly recommend researching each coin you desire to purchase to reduce the risk of being exposed to fraud. I have heard many stories of people just buying an altcoin because it was performing well, and the coin disappears. Further, there is no one to contact to file a complaint. Even in this space, bad people exist, and they want to deceive you to take your money.

Okay, I feel better with the warning. Now we know that to start purchasing digital, you must buy into the primary space: Bitcoin, Ethereum, and Litecoin. You can go to the altcoin realm from there, only if you choose to do so. It is not necessary. Everyone, from retail investors to hedge fund managers, are joining the digital space. But why? What is so special about investing in the digital space? It may help to explain a little about what digital currency is. From this point on, I will use Bitcoin as an example. It is the most popular, and many investors are diversifying their managed portfolios here.

Bitcoin is purely digital, and it must be mined and is limited in quantity, which gives it its value. In the beginning (around 2009), Bitcoin was created, or mined, using computer code and a lot of fairy dust (just kidding… but only about the fairy dust, not the computer code).

$IDE NOTE: Bitcoin is mined by using an incorruptible computer code that records a proof of work (PoW) system. With the use of this special code and using special graphics and central processing units (GPU/CPU), this creates and adds the mined coin to the blockchain. Blockchain technology is a public ledger that records Bitcoin transactions. Satoshi Nakamoto is the name used as the developer of this technology. It is a mystery, to this day, who this person (or group) is.

The first Bitcoin was valued at $1 U.S. dollar. But the creation of a Bitcoin requires special computers, software, and a lot of electrical energy… A LOT. To create one Bitcoin cost a lot more than what it was initially worth. There are many variables to the creation costs, but it was around $10,000 per coin in the beginning. Now there are mining facilities that are typically located in areas around the world that have inexpensive energy. Also, by design of the code, Bitcoin is limited, meaning there is not an infinite amount of Bitcoin, unlike fiat currency. Through the mining process, there is a limit of 21 million coins that can be mined. No additional coins can be made. As of early 2023, the coins have not yet been mined to this limit. Having a limit set on the quantity gives it the scarcity of gold, as it, too, is limited on the amount that has been mined. This gives the holder of Bitcoin protection from devaluation that occurs naturally with fiat currencies.

But keep in mind, Bitcoin is not legal tender for most nations. In September 2021, the first nation to adopt Bitcoin as legal tender was the Republic of El Salvador. Other countries are considering Bitcoin as legal tender as well, such as: the Republic of Honduras, the Republic of Panama, and the Republic of Paraguay. Despite that it is not legal tender in most countries, it can be used anywhere people or businesses are willing to make a transaction. It is an agreement between the two parties performing the exchange. This is called 'peer to peer' transactions. It does not require a central bank to be in the middle, therefore earning the title of "The People's Money."

Bitcoin cannot be duplicated or counterfeited, as it uses blockchain technology. Trust in Bitcoin is increasing exponentially, especially in countries with failing currencies, such as Argentina and Venezuela. And it is evident that fund managers are investing large portions of their portfolios into this space as well.

What are the downsides to decentralized money? Well, try paying your taxes with it. It is not acceptable tender to most governmental entities, and to use it to pay your taxes, you will be forced to exchange your Bitcoin to fiat currency first.

Because Bitcoin is digital, you may be wondering what happens if the internet goes down. Obviously, Bitcoin will not work if this happens, but it is deemed safe, and will be there, waiting for you when power is restored. However, Bitcoin did not help anyone in Puerto Rico when the island was without power for months after being devastated by Hurricane Maria in 2017. No electricity equals no Bitcoin. On top of that, Bitcoin is illegal to use in some countries, including China, Russia, Colombia, Vietnam, and Ecuador. Your Bitcoin cannot be used there.

Most governments around the world are wrapped up in the central banking system, and support of Bitcoin or decentralized currencies is now threatening the establishments. After learning about these central banks and how they basically control the world, do you really think they would do something that would give up control and power to the people's money? Another reminder: "He who controls the gold controls the world."

The central banks can easily change or create new laws to discourage or make the use of Bitcoin illegal. The U.S. Government has already implemented laws to tax any gains made from digital currency. I ask again, do you think the central banks will give up control of the money to a people's money? If you answered yes, please go back to page one and start over (just kidding).

Never forget that the bankers at the top do not think like you and me. They do not want to give up control of the money, for if you control the money, you control the people.

At this point in time, Bitcoin is mostly used as an investment vehicle. At its creation, it was difficult to get $1 USD for one coin. In 2017, Bitcoin made it to the $20,000 USD mark and then came crashing down to under $5,000. By October 2020, it was attempting to break $25,000, and in March 2021, it broke the $60,000 mark. Since that high mark, Bitcoin has been volatile sliding back down to $33,000 in July and bouncing around the mid-$40,000 mark in the first week of August 2021. In October 2021, Bitcoin broke its all-time high of $66,999 and has held steady in the low $60,000 range into November 2021. Then 2022 was a year of decline as it slowly fell to around $17,000. Eventually, as more and more of the big money handlers invest in Bitcoin, it will begin to be less volatile and become safer for you and me to enter this space.

The central banks are seeing the threat of the common people's fortunes rising with their own currency and are developing ways to combat Bitcoin and other cryptocurrency. Rumor has it that there will be a Fedcoin, or digital dollar, that is set to take over the world reserve currency status. Just imagine that once enacted, your government will know every transaction you will make, perhaps even put restrictions on what you can buy based on health or legality, perhaps even for rationing purposes. The U.S. government will be able to directly tax your spending on everything you purchase. Controls that are even more devious could likely be put into place. Let your imagination run with this thought.

You may be saying to yourself that this is probably only going to happen way down the road, and you don't need to be concerned about it now. Did you know that the U.S. Congress already tried to sneak in the Act to approve this in the U.S. in the March 2020 CARES Act? It was pulled out, but rest assured, it is already written and ready to be voted into law.

Fun Internet Search: Look up "Financial Protections and Assistance for America's Consumers, States, Businesses, and Vulnerable Populations Act. H.R. 6321."

All the government is waiting for is an opportunity. Over time, once passed, this Fedcoin currency should eliminate the need of your local banks, and the Federal Reserve will be your bank. Not so far off now, is it?

Also, in the U.S., did you notice that there was a change (pennies, nickels, dimes, and quarters) shortage in 2020? Did you notice the media reporting how the COVID-19 virus could survive on the surface of currency? Businesses began shifting to cashless transactions because of this concern, as well as to reduce the spreading of the virus. Is it possible to believe that these are mental tactics in preparing you to accept the government form of digital currency? Governments are controlled by the banking system and will have laws written to benefit their own currency. Whether or not they will be successful in suppressing decentralized currency remains to be seen, and I am not predicting either way. I am just warning you to be aware of the fight to come for dominance.

$
PLAIN & SIMPLE BREAKDOWN

The main takeaway from this chapter is that we are rapidly entering a digital currency era. I see a collision course in the future between the decentralized (people's money) currency and centralized (central banks and Federal Reserve Bank) currency. They will attempt to convince you that your life will be easier with the convenience of a central bank currency, not to be mistaken for the de-centralized coins. Never lose sight that any CBDC is still fiat just like the fiat paper currency that is printed.

That should always be in the back of your mind while navigating in the digital world. Governments enjoy power, and they get power through money. If they lose control over money, they will lose their power. All a government will have to do is shut off the decentralized currency, and the value will be zero. Will it happen? I cannot say, but digital currency is not physical, right? What I will say is that this scenario will not materialize without a fight. If history proves a predictor of the future, remember, governments do not relinquish control willingly.

CHAPTER 9

GLOBAL CURRENCY

"Who controls the food supply controls the people;
who controls the energy can control whole continents;
who controls money can control the world."
— **Henry Kissinger** (1923-), 56th United States Secretary of State, Politician,
Diplomat, Geopolitical Consultant

Have you ever thought how nice it would be to have one monetary unit and have it used equally in every country and with every person across the globe? I remember going to Panama while in the U.S. Air Force, and I was able to use the U.S. dollar everywhere in that country, as it was their currency too. Their coins were Panamanian, though, but very similar to the U.S. coins. I realize now that the Panamanian government used the U.S. dollar to stabilize their own economy, which may have been a smart move, especially for international trade.

However, let's not go too deep into the Panamanian economy here. Rather, this chapter is designed to inform you of a bigger agenda. This agenda originates from the IMF, short for International Monetary Fund. This may sound uninteresting to an entry level financial wizard such as yourself, but store this in your brain, as there is a good chance you will become very familiar with it in the future.

The IMF was born out of the 1945 Bretton Woods Conference. The IMF is a financial organization that has almost 200 countries as members, and they contribute money to the IMF and manage it as cash reserves. When countries encounter economic stress or financial crises, the IMF will step in and loan money to them. The currency that is issued by the IMF is called SDR, or special drawing rights, and it is considered as a type of international monetary reserve. The value of the SDR is calculated based on several major currencies, such as the U.S. dollar, the euro, the Japanese yen, the British pound, and the Chinese yuan.

Here is where this is leading you to: There is a push from the IMF to create its own cryptocurrency. Just know that this is getting traction as well. They are calling it central bank digital currency (CBDC). They have challenges to overcome, but they are aggressively working through them.

$ $

PLAIN & SIMPLE BREAKDOWN

The key takeaway on this subject is that there is a push for cryptocurrency by many bankers, including the Federal Reserve Bank. This is a race, and the ones who win will run the world. Think about it: The Federal Reserve Bank funding the U.S. dollar has made the U.S. the wealthiest nation in the world for seventy-five years. How else can a country that exports very little and consumes very much be prosperous? Hopefully, you are thinking, *Free money.* Now, with that simple wisdom, who does not want this power for the next seventy-five years or more? Who will be the last bank standing? Will it be the Federal Reserve Bank and their Fedcoin? How about the IMF and their CBDC? Maybe even Bitcoin will rise up and overrule all? Do not forget the Chinese, as they are looking for that control as well with the digital yuan. This can go many directions. These are only a few of the strongest possibilities.

CHAPTER 10

BANKING IN THE U.S.A.

"If the American people ever allow private banks to control the issue of their currency, first by inflation, then by deflation, the banks and corporations that will grow up around [the banks] will deprive the people of all property, until their children wake up homeless on the continent their fathers conquered. The issuing power should be taken from the banks and restored to the people, to whom it properly belongs."
— **Thomas Jefferson** (1743-1826), American statesman, diplomat, lawyer, slaveholder, architect, musician, philosopher, Founding Father and Third President of the United States

Have you ever thought about banking and how it works? No matter where on this planet you live, you were probably taught some basic information, like me, about your local bank. Compare your mental notes with mine by picturing the bank in your town or neighborhood. I grew up believing that my bank was a place to take my money to make it grow. I do not recall the interest earned on a savings account, but I believe it was greater than four percent.

To a child, that meant for each dollar deposited would earn four cents in a year. Not bad for back then, as fiat currency still had some sort of value. But did you ever ask yourself why your bank was giving you money back?

I was taught that if people of a community deposited their savings, then the bank would loan the deposit out at a higher interest rate. From the loan, the bank makes a little, and the savers (or depositors) would be paid their dividends as well. Back then, the interest rate on a mortgage was over ten percent. This makes sense, right? It seems like a legitimate business. This is not a bad model, as the bank makes money, the saver makes money, and the money loaned is used to promote growth or improvement in the community. Winner, winner, chicken dinner.

Do you want to know the truth regarding today's banking system? For some reason, people still believe in the model described, but it could not be further from truth. First, I want to remind you about how fiat currency is created. All currency is debt and is loaned into existence. We all agree to this, right? Now, there are some other cogs to this sprocket to consider.

In the chapter about the Fed and central banks, I described how fractional reserve banking works. Recall that if a person or a business is seeking a loan from the bank, the bank is required to have a tenth of that loan on hand or available. Please understand that upon approval of a loan the bank funds, they only need to have ten percent in reserves. Have you begun to wonder where the other ninety percent comes from? Do you give up? It is created from thin air. So, the money you have in savings is multiplied by ten to loan out to others. Confused? Are you seeing the scam? If not, allow me to peel the onion another layer.

The bank, through lending, creates digits on the computer (not physical cash) and is able to charge interest on that balance that is loaned. The way I see it, they are licensed to counterfeit. Wait... is that too harsh?

I am trying to understand why we as a people cannot print money and use it. If we did, we would be charged as criminals, right? I do not think anyone questions this practice, because it allows us to obtain the funds that we need for whatever purpose is important to us. Therefore, the bank gets a pass from the public.

$URPRI$E! You may recall that Federal Reserve Board reduced the reserve requirement ratios to zero percent, effective March 26, 2020. This action eliminated reserve requirements for all depository institutions indefinitely. So, the banks no longer are required to have the ten percent they once needed to make a loan. Incredible, isn't it, to be able to create something (currency) from nothing and make more currency from this product by charging the borrower interest on the loan?

Bank balance sheets are an extremely confusing topic to me. In keeping with the spirit of this plain and simple book, you need to, at a minimum, understand what a balance sheet is. You will also need this basic understanding once you ascend your way up the financial ladder.

A balance sheet is simply a sheet that has two columns titled "Assets" and "Liabilities." Do not let me lose you on this: Assets are things you own that put money in your pocket, and liabilities do the opposite by taking money out. The goal should be to have more assets than liabilities. Banks have the same, but sometimes money is in both columns, and it is hard to follow. For example, a deposit could be a liability, while a loan could be an asset, all considered in a different context.

Why am I even telling you this? Ready?

Banks have laws to follow, meaning that they will need to cover their obligations every day, and sometimes they may overextend themselves.

When they do, they need to keep things on the up-and-up, and they lend each other funds to stay in the black (positive balances). Their balance sheets will back up their loans with their assets, and they are constantly traded between each other all the time. The terms of the loans can be for one night, or all the way up to several months. As you may imagine, it can get super crazy. If things go haywire, like bad assets, sometimes called junk or toxic, then the banks stop lending to each other. Then what?

In comes the repo market. That is where all these transactions take place. The repo market involves clearing houses and primary dealers overseen by the Federal Reserve. The repo market made the news in September 2019, but it appeared that no one I knew paid any mind to the news as they did not have car loans, or they were current on the loan payment and did not worry about a repossession. But it seemed that there was no interest among us common folks, because there was no understanding to what was taking place.

No, "repo" does not imply repossession of any kind. It stands for repurchase agreement, and it's a simple form of short-term borrowing for dealers (like banks) in government securities.

Let's get back on a track of simplicity now, and what I want you to know is that this was the straw that broke the camel's back. The Federal Reserve Bank and central banks have entered unchartered financial territory. In the financial world, the Fed has made many monetary promises to keep the economy thriving, as reflected in the stock market. The market is higher than ever now, isn't it?

The Fed and central banks have committed to becoming the "buyer of last resort." What this means, at a non-technical level, is that they will make more currency available to keep any bank from collapsing. Banks collapse due to risky loans or investments they have made. When the corporations default or private borrowers default, the Fed and central banks create more currency to keep the failing banks open. They have committed to doing whatever it takes even if that means creating more fake money. This is what we saw during the Great Financial Crisis of 2008. We were sold that the US commercial banks were "too big to fail" and that they needed to be 'bailed out.' And that is what happened, to the tune of $700 billion that was authorized by the US Congress through the Troubled Assets Relief Program (TARP).

In 2010, the U.S. Congress passed the Dodd-Frank Wall Street Reform and Consumer Act in response to the Great Financial Crisis, to fix things so that this collapse would never happen again by making the financial industry safer for consumers and taxpayers. One of the items to highlight here is the new term "Bail-In" not to be confused with "Bail-Out." Well, what does this mean to you and me? What this means is, if a depositor has more than $250,000 (the FDIC insured amount) in an institution, that excess is now available for the bank to use in the event of it failing. Yes, you loaned the currency to them and now they can use it to pay their creditors. The central banks around the world are implementing this already. Just ask anyone who had money in the banks of Greece around 2013. Something to consider if this applies to you.

Before moving on, I want to give you the pieces to this peculiar puzzle. Due to the global pandemic, we have all experienced some sort of lockdown. Some places have had it worse than others. This lockdown affected tourism and hospitality, manufacturing, the food and beverage industry, and the performing arts to name a few. With these lockdowns came a loss of employment of, perhaps, billions of people throughout the world. This all has an effect on the payments due to the banks, because they lent to these businesses that are now distressed. Any bank can withstand a few businesses going under. That is normal and expected. What is way out of the norm is when a tsunami of businesses go under and cannot pay. Banks are not prepared for this.

If this is true, if banks truly were not prepared for all these businesses to discontinue payments, then how are banks open and still doing business?

Let's go back to the conversation of the Fed and central banks. Understand that this is a high-level explanation, but through bond purchasing, the central banks and Fed end up owning many assets by creating fake money. At first, they were contributing billions of U.S. dollars to the repo market. These institutions claimed it to be a short-term fix for a couple of weeks. Then they committed more money and extended it for another month. Then they again committed more money and extended it out to January 2020.

Then the pandemic of 2020 arrived, and it was forgotten. Hmm... conspiracy theory? You be the judge. The timing couldn't be better, though. I do know that the Federal Reserve has since been contributing trillions of dollars and has stated that there are no limits to its purchasing of bonds. This move explains how so many folks could be out of work, yet the stock market continued to reach all-time highs.

$ $
PLAIN & SIMPLE BREAKDOWN

What I want you to take from this chapter is that we operate in an unfair banking system. There is a group of central banks that have somehow created a financial system in which the banks create money from nothing, and we must use it and pay the banks for its use. If you hold a currency note, regardless of country of issue, it is debt. It will always be debt.

What the central banks have done in the time of a crisis is just create more debt. Imagine you as an individual who is trying to get out of debt. Would you think that borrowing a lot more money is the sound path of getting out of debt? No. It is common sense to any of us that this is not possible. The craziest thing about all of this is being able to exchange fiat debt (fake) for real assets, and that is what the Fed and central banks are doing. Could you buy real assets with fake money? YES. Think land (your home), precious metals, and cryptocurrencies (because they are not part of the central banking system).

CHAPTER 11

CAUGHT IN THE MIDDLE

"By a continuing process of inflation, government can confiscate, secretly and unobserved, an important part of the wealth of their citizens."
— **John Maynard Keynes** (1883-1946), English Economist and thought leader of Keynesian Economics)

Anyone in any part of the world should have a basic foundational understanding about inflationary terms, because they go hand in hand with the currency you have in your pocket, work for, and spend. The following terms are most commonly used to describe an economy, and the following discussion on this topic will stay in plain and simple terms. I want to make understandable how inflation affects a person's purchasing power. These inflationary conditions are good for some and bad for others. *How is that?* you ask.

First, let us begin with a general definition of inflation. Merriam-Webster defines it as "a continuing rise in the general price level usually attributed to an increase in the volume of money and credit relative to available goods and services." I remember when I went to the grocery store as a child and was told that the entire cart full of groceries was around $20. Then as time went on, it was three quarters of the cart for the same amount, and eventually only half the cart for $20. Today, I am lucky if I can get a small plastic bag of groceries for that amount. That is inflation to the ordinary person; the cost of the goods has gone up.

Now, after you've ventured through the previous chapters, here is a vital fact: Inflation happens when the value of the currency diminishes. Do not forget that all currency is fiat. And how does fiat perform over time? This is what I explained in the gold and silver values overview in an earlier chapter. Back to the measuring part... the government selects certain common goods in the U.S. and averages them out. This is done over small periods of time and provides a statistic on how the economy is performing. This is called the CPI, for Consumer Price Index.

Second, you need an understanding of deflation, which is the opposite of inflation. The prices of the same items go down, and the currency used has an increase in its value. Normally, this is caused by a contraction of money supply and/or credit in the economy. This would be a great scenario for everyone if we were all paid the same and prices went down. However, it doesn't work that way.

Third, we have stagflation: The word "stag" must mean stagnant. And that's what it becomes. Stagflation is slow economic growth, combined with relatively high unemployment. At the same time, prices of goods and services still rise. You are probably thinking right now that this does not make sense. If people make less (or no) money, they cannot purchase as much. Therefore, sales of goods are less and should push prices down. Exactly. So, how does stagflation enter the room? One way is an increase in money supply pushed out to the population through welfare programs or stimulus programs. There is no productivity for the money individuals received.

Since we are discussing money supply, I want to be certain that you have a plain and simple understanding of the fiat system. Remember, in a fiat system, there are no restrictions on how much money is in the economy. This power to create more fiat money resides with the great and wonderful bankers, who are entrusted with making these especially important decisions.

I like to use this simple explanation regarding money and how supply affects your purchasing power. First, imagine an economy that has only 100 units in it (it could be a dollar, euro, real, peso, or anything else). Now, of those 100 units, you have one. What share in percentage points do you have of this economy? Did you come up with one percent? Good.

Now, our bankers decide that there is not enough money in the economy, and they feel that it now needs 200 units. If you still have that one unit, what does that mean for you after the increase? What do you have? Still the one percent? Not so fast. You now have half a percent. Your value was just reduced by half. And here's the topper: You do not work less or need fewer goods or services. Does that seem fair? Welcome to inflation.

Inflation happens in a fiat monetary system, simply by design. As a reminder, all fiat is debt. It must be loaned into existence. As more loans are given, more fiat enters the financial system. As more fiat is added, the fiat that has already been created becomes worth less. When it is worth less, your purchasing power is decreased. When purchasing power is decreased, you need more fiat to buy the same items.

This becomes a vicious cycle, and the only thing that becomes more affordable is the fiat that was loaned earlier in time. Therefore, you may hear that "they are going to inflate this away." What that means is, if you have spent today's money and pay it back with tomorrow's money, well, you get more value right now than tomorrow, because the money will normally be worth less tomorrow (or is it worthless?). Let me clear this up with an example.

In the debt-based monetary system we all live in, fiat currency loses its value as time marches on. If you were to borrow currency today and pay it back over several years into the future, that loan will be repaid with less-valued currency. Now, I am not recommending going into debt based on this example, as other factors need to be considered: What is the purpose of the loan? Is it for an asset or liability? What about the interest charged for the loan? Is it high or low? Can the asset service the loan obligation?

When considering loans, will the interest be less than the inflation rate? When it is less, you should be able to see the advantages to borrowing. A rule of thumb is that credit card debt is NEVER a good bet against inflation.

Is it possible to get into hyperinflation? What is that? Hyperinflation is simply inflation that is out of control. The central banks will have lost control of interest rates, and they are dumping money into the economy at record paces. Has it happened? Yes. Good examples of this can been seen in Germany's Wiemar Republic (early 1920s), then more recently in Venezuela, Zimbabwe, and Lebanon (in 2021), among others.

This is the expectancy of any fiat currency: its value will inevitably depreciate to zero. I encourage you to investigate these countries' hyperinflation conditions. It affects virtually everyone in these countries, unless they are part of the elite group running the country or have purchased assets.

What about the U.S. dollar then? Can it be subject to hyperinflation? My short answer is yes, but it is different than the other countries that have fallen. The Federal Reserve Bank loaned trillions of U.S. dollars in 2020, with no end in sight. Yet the dollar seems to hold on without hyperinflation creeping in.

I know there is a complex explanation to this, so I will not even attempt to go there. Let us keep this plain and simple. From my understanding, the world reserve currency status that the U.S. dollar enjoys has thus far insulated it from hyperinflation. That has allowed the out-of-control creation of money that we are all witnessing. Since all the other nations' currency are coupled with the U.S. dollar, they end up purchasing more U.S. dollars around the world. They must do this to purchase oil and repay loans that are denominated in the U.S. dollar. This results in giving the dollar strength. You can say that the U.S. dollar is the cleanest shirt in the dirty clothes hamper.

I do not think anyone knows how far this expansion of money supply can be taken without breaking the entire financial system. But it sure seems that the institutions and the elites are trying to find that limit or tipping point. Watch out for the irresponsible acts of our bankers for after all, 40% of the U.S. dollar money supply was printed from 2020-2022.

This should make one wonder if the prices of goods and services will increase. Well, in 2022 the U.S. has experienced 40-year highs in the CPI every month! I bet no one saw this coming, as you can see how the politicians are pointing fingers at everyone except for themselves.

Remember the unit scenario I explained earlier; when money is worth zero, it does not matter how much you have. For example, if you had $1,000,000 and multiplied it by zero, it equals zero. No matter the direction of the economy, you will be caught in the middle.

$ $

PLAIN & SIMPLE BREAKDOWN

Hopefully, this chapter made it clear that education regarding inflation will help you make better financial decisions for the future. The road we all are being led down ends in a bad destination but knowing what is to come will allow you to prepare. Please do not think you will be able to prepare after the storm has arrived. Perhaps you have very little money and feel helpless due to the cost of precious metals and real estate. Don't.

Think of inflation in terms of your day-to-day needs and start purchasing things that will not perish "as you shop." Buy things with today's purchasing power with an eye toward items you will need tomorrow. Your new understanding that we live in a monetary system that is designed to fail is a concept that many will never see. I think, at this point in the book, you should be starting to see this and see the potential destruction that could be in store for many unsuspecting people.

At least you now understand that any money you save in a bank account is declining in purchasing power. The longer it stays there, the weaker it becomes. The good news is that there are steps you can take that can maximize your finances and improve the survivability of this deteriorating fiat monetary system. Replicating the wealthy is one way of protecting yourself. They are purchasing something of value now (assets) to be able to exchange for fiat later. Perhaps you could plan to do the same?

CHAPTER 12

ECONOMIC THEORIES

"I see in the near future a crisis approaching that unnerves me and causes me to tremble for the safety of my country... corporations have been enthroned and an era of corruption in high places will follow, and the money power of the country will endeavor to prolong its reign by working upon the prejudices of the people until all wealth is aggregated in a few hands and the Republic is destroyed."
— **Abraham Lincoln** (1809-1865), 16th President of the United States

Having to study economic theories in college was a real snoozer for me. But now, I wish I had paid a little more attention to this subject. I will add that what is revealed in this chapter is necessary, but, as I stated before, we will keep this plain and simple. Do not panic. Just keep reading.

We will discuss only a few of the theories I've learned about that have any sort of relevance to the ordinary person. These will give you an understanding that makes sense and adds to your newly learned knowledge. The theories I am going to introduce to you are the Cantillon Effect, Keynesian Theory, and Modern Monetary Theory (M-M-T).

Richard Cantillon was an Irish-French economist, who wrote an essay regarding economic theory in the early to mid-eighteenth century. To keep this quite simple, it basically explains that the recipients of created fiat currency are the ones who benefit the most from the currency's value. *Huh?* Here is another way to say it: The people closest to the money printer receive the most benefit of the currency.

Here is how that works out: When currency is created (talking about fiat), it must be loaned into the economy. The recipients of this currency use it at its full value. As we learned earlier, any additional currency injected into the economy creates inflation, and currency loses its value, right? Well, as the currency is used (by spending), it trickles down to those further away from the printer, all while the currency loses its purchasing power to the ones now holding it. As they spend, it loses more value and, ultimately, as it gets to the folks furthest from the printer, they now have inflated currency that has very little purchasing power compared to the amount of purchasing power the ones at the top—those first to receive it—had when the currency was more valuable. Because this effect is in play today, we witness enormously powerful people and companies or governments position themselves to be next in line to the printing presses (of course, this is a figure of speech). These folks have coined the term "Cantillionaires."

John Maynard Keynes describes Keynesian economics. He wrote about this in his book *The General Theory of Employment, Interest and Money,* when the United States was recovering from the Great Depression in the 1930s. His explanation should sound remarkably familiar to what most of us in the world are bearing witness to in today's economy. He explains how economic output is influenced by aggregate demand (total spending in the economy).

To start with, he held this viewpoint: "In the long run, we are all dead." This should lead you to think that the end is not good, but it does not matter, because we will die. In a fiat currency system, Keynesian economics states that the more spending there is, the more productive the economy will become. This is a great model until something upsets it, like a recession. In a recession, there is less demand for goods and services, because people are not comfortable with spending, and they hold back their spending. With the decrease in demand of goods and services, more people will be producing less and therefore will either have their pay reduced or maybe even lose their jobs.

Now enter the government. Politicians do not want this to happen and will begin to stimulate by purchasing goods and services or directly sending money into the economy for people to spend. This sounds great, but there is a price to pay, and usually it will come in the form of higher taxes and inflation resulting in reduced purchasing power.

During depressions and recessions, when government spending is their answer to correction, the result is more debt that must be repaid. The additional burden placed on the taxpayers for this debt now goes back to the government instead of the possible goods and services of the economy. It creates a tailspin that eventually gets out of control. Keynes understood this from his quote that we are all going to die. I have heard financial teachers say, "It works until it doesn't." Profound.

Most of the developed nations of today's world (countries that belong to the central bank system) use these principles and wrap them neatly in a package they call Modern Monetary Theory (M-M-T). The fun meaning is: More Money Today. By design, this is extraordinarily complex, but let us learn it from 40,000 feet. From that high up, we can see it in its basic form and what it is supposed to do.

The central banks, beginning with the Federal Reserve, need to protect the fake currency's value, and to do that they need to monitor various data points as they relate to the economy. And as a solution to problems that arise, they have tools to correct these problems. What are these data points, you may wonder?

From our viewpoint, the data point is primarily consumer inflation. The central banks monitor the CPI and attempt to control this at an annual rate of 2%. Envision driving a car in a hilly area; imagine what you have to do to maintain a certain speed. If you go uphill, you must apply more of the throttle, and to drive on level terrain, all you have to do is hold the throttle in its position. When you go downhill, normally you ease back on the throttle. That is what the central banks do to manage inflation, but when inflation is rising, they must respond, normally by increasing interest rates and use quantitative tightening (QT). QT reduces the Fed's balance sheet. In plain and simple terms: bank reserves are removed from the banking system.

Test Question: How does currency enter our economy?
Answer: A+ if you said *through lending*.

Now, if consumer inflation is going the way they want, the central banks do nothing. And if inflation is stagnant, then the central banks will lower interest rates and use quantitative easing (QE). QE creates more currency (technically bank reserves), and it is added to the economy.

Test Question: What happens to existing currency when the central banks remove currency from the economy?
Answer: Excellent. I am positive that you said: *the value will increase*.

Now, you are probably asking yourself questions like, how low can they lower the interest rates? Or, how low are they right now? Can interest rates go into negative territory? How can they just create currency to put into the economy? How about, where does the currency go when it is removed from the economy? Can I have it?

You should check where your country's central bank is for their lending rates. Many of them have entered the negative territory. The chairman of the Federal Reserve Bank stated in 2020 they do not plan to go beyond zero percent over the next few years. I hope this concerns you in regard to your currency. Low interest rates may be great for those borrowing, but consider your savings, if you have any, as there is no, or extraordinarily little, return on your deposits. As a matter of fact, it may cost you currency to save.

$ PLAIN & SIMPLE BREAKDOWN

What you should take away regarding these economic theories is that it's important for you to see the plan and behaviors of those who control the currency. We now have a basic understanding of fiat and what the value is. Fiat is fake, and our economies are fake. The bankers already know that, and they need to keep the economies operating through manipulation. They manipulate money supply and interest rates to do so. These are clues for us to watch and to know what is coming, financially, based on the actions the central banks take.

For example, if they are adding to the currency supply, you now know that consumer inflation is on its way. If they decrease interest rates, you now know that they are trying to promote more lending, as the economy is becoming sluggish. You also now know that when the interest rates go to zero or less than zero percent, there are serious problems with the economy, and you should take action for yourself and your family.

CHAPTER 13

THE GREAT RESET

"The stupidity of the average man will permit the oligarch, whether economic or political, to hide his real purposes from the scrutiny of his fellows and to withdraw his activities from effective control. Since it is impossible to count on enough moral goodwill among those who possess irresponsible power to sacrifice it for the good of the whole, it must be destroyed by coercive methods, and these will always run the peril of introducing new forms of injustice in place of those abolished."
— **Reinhold Niebuhr** (1892-1971), American Reformed Theologian Ethicist, Recipient of the Presidential Medal of Freedom

For many years, I had the pleasure of being an aircraft mechanic and was blessed to work the big jets with a lot of technology built into them. From time to time, an odd malfunction arose, and an easy repair was to open a circuit breaker for the failed system and to push it back in. That reset the computer, and all was back to normal.

Sometimes though, so many malfunctions happened at once that I would have to shut down the entire aircraft and, at times, disconnect the battery. Now, in the aviation world, this was a "great reset" for the aircraft. Can you imagine being a passenger in your seat, ready to fly, and the captain announces that they must reset the aircraft? Yikes. I have had that happened to me, and I knew it would be fine, but the other passengers around me seemed a bit nervous. They just did not understand what was going on.

I do not want you to be one of these passengers. There is a reason for you to be reading this book, and I am sure you have many questions and observations about money by now. I would like to reinforce to you that human emotions are a major influence of our money system, too. Always keep that tidbit of information in the back of your mind.

I do not want to make this book political, nor do I aim to sway your thoughts in any direction. However, because governments are institutions and wield enormous power, it is almost impossible to keep politics out of a discussion about money. Since governments have given financial control to the central banks, politics and every aspect of monetary systems have become linked. I only mention this, because there are many uprisings around the world, and it seems there is also a presence that aims to promote our differences.

There is a saying: "Divide and conquer." This is a tactic used in battle, used in sports, and used in business. This technique is now being used in society in the form of ethnicity, wealth classes, and even sexuality. Division is promoted at every angle. Have you ever thought about why? I have and let me share what I have come up with: It's the reason I'm writing this book. The monetary system is broken, and the institutions and the elite don't want the general public to pay attention to it. The tried-and-true method to distract, by division, leads us to attack one another instead of attacking the ones who are controlling the monetary system.

I recently saw a cartoon that had a king who looked worried as he overlooked his subjects surrounding his castle. They were very angry (probably because of his monetary policies). Half of them had pitchforks, and the other half had torches. He was worried because he knew their anger was directed toward him. The king had an advisor who said to him, as they overlooked the angry mob, "Oh, you don't need to fight them. You just need to convince the pitchfork people that the torch people want to take away their pitchforks."

You may ask what this has to do with a reset. Remember the division. Are our differences amplified to have us focus on each other rather than the king (or bankers)? Think about that for a minute. What are they keeping us from seeing?

Have you ever heard of the Hegelian Dialectic? It is an interpretive method used to guide societies in a particular direction or belief. This is my simple explanation: First, an entity (usually government) creates a problem. Second, there is a reaction to the problem. Third, the same entity creates a solution. This method has been used over and over throughout history to achieve a particular goal. In the case of the great reset, most of us cannot see the need of a monetary reset. I want to remind you that the monetary system is at the end of the cycle. Not only do you now know this, but the central banks have known this for some time as well. Also, the banks want to remain in control of it all.

And here we all are. The banks know the fiat is worthless (problem), and they know that soon you will be aware of this and demand change and justice (reaction). Then they will introduce the solution to our money problems. No one knows what the solution is or will be. We are not to this point just yet. Most people in the world do not even know that there is a problem, as they are kept distracted with pandemic reactions, mass immigrations, or a physical war. I am willing to wager that the solution will not benefit us. What do you think?

My first indication of a reset is just hearing this as a new buzzword during my journey in the financial realm. Along with that, I also started to hear about a debt jubilee. *Great*, I thought, *something else I must look up.* A debt jubilee is in the bible, and it's when a debtor is forgiven of their debts after seven years. So, in today's market, it must mean a forgiveness of debt.

Now settle down. Ask yourself first, whose debts? What will it cost? Or, better yet, what must be given in return to be forgiven? This is something to watch for, as it is possible to carry out a jubilee. Do you remember that all currency used today was made from nothing? But those who forgive the debt will leverage that to get what *they* want. I can assure you this much is true.

I urge you to understand that this is just a theory, and one should always practice financial responsibility, especially when it comes to indebtedness. Governments, on the other hand, are spending at record levels and have no end in sight. By the end of 2022, the United States went more than $31.4 trillion in government debt, and spending is not slowing at all. As a matter of fact, the American politicians are planning on spending much, much more. I can state with near certainty that there is not a plan to repay this debt. So, naturally, one can deduce that this must be reset before it collapses. This is only one nation. Just imagine what the world debt looks like.

Personal debt, like home mortgages, credit cards, and auto loans, has also reached levels that are seemingly impossible to repay. At this time, it is reported to be over 24 trillion dollars in the United States alone. And many people were not working at the start of the pandemic crisis in 2020 and into 2021, which only perpetuates the debt repayment problem. Add to this how many people are living paycheck to paycheck before this inflation kicked into high gear and are trying to find ways to keep up with the pace. Some have the luxury of credit cards or loans. And that is the preferred choice when there is work. What happens when the recession arrives to the scene? Many who haven't prepared may lose their jobs. And that starts the nose dive when the paychecks stop. The bills do not get paid, then the collector starts collecting. Oh, this brings up bad memories for me. When this is isolated to a few families, the economy can handle it, but when it happens to the masses, almost everyone is affected. When the debts can no longer be serviced on such a massive scale, they, too, will more than likely initiate a crash of the financial system. Now, what I am reading about the personal debt forgiveness would be that you would forfeit any property you own in return to be debt free. But you should know already, there are no free lunches.

Something else to keep your eye on is the World Economic Forum (WEF). They are the International Organization for Public-Private Cooperation. The forum engages the foremost political, business, and cultural leaders of society to shape global, regional, and industrial agendas. Yes, they have plans for the world.

One of their latest economic objectives is seen in the promotion of their new tag line: "You will own nothing and be happy." Their economic model describes a lifestyle in which we will not even have a house but share homes with each other. If you need something, you can rent it, then return it when you are done. For spending, they want to give you an allowance called Universal Basic Income (UBI).

There is much more to this plan, and the WEF is promoting all of this now with an implementation start date of around 2030. This is their idea of a great reset. Does it align with your plans? It may sound good to many people, because it involves fewer expenses and the promise of no work for most. How do you think they could usher this in? Perhaps a financial crisis? Perhaps a health crisis?

$
PLAIN & SIMPLE BREAKDOWN

Here is what you need to know regarding a great reset: No one really knows how it will happen, nor does anyone know whom it will affect. More than likely, it will affect all of us ordinary people trapped in this debt-based monetary system. My only intent is to make sure you, as my new friend, know what to watch for so you can avoid the shenanigans these bankers impose on us. They want us to not know or understand their business, so that they remain in control. Be on the lookout so that the great reset doesn't catch you by surprise. How can you counter this right now? Watch your debt levels. Try not to incur any unnecessary debt for the time being. Also, position yourself to acquire assets without going into debt. Debt is a bondage that we each need to shed. Buyer beware.

CHAPTER 14

SPEED ROUND

"Ignorance is not bliss. Ignorance is poverty.
Ignorance is devastation. Ignorance is tragedy.
And ignorance is illness. It all stems from ignorance."
—**Jim Rohn** (1930-2009), American Entrepreneur,
Author and Motivational Speaker

This is a chapter of bits and pieces. There are several topics that everyone should know about, but do not require a deep dive. I do encourage you to research all (or some) of them as you seek out more understanding. There is no specific order of importance, and they are explained in a way that I have come to understand them. Ready?

Velocity of Money (M2V)

There is a measurement that is used to assist in determining the health of an economy. This term is "velocity of money." Just like the name, it measures the speed of money. What is amazing about this is how money is multiplied exponentially as it is used through an economy. Well, that was easy to explain, right? Okay, it means more, and there is a story that helped with the understanding of this term.

A businessman was driving to a town for a meeting and had a tire blowout just outside the town. As he began to replace the tire with the spare, he realized that his jack was missing, and he could not replace the tire. He caught a ride into town so he could borrow a jack to change the tire. At the local auto repair shop, they had a tool loaner program, and they loaned him a jack for a $100 cash deposit that would be refunded when he returned the jack. He gave the owner a $100 bill that he had tucked away in his wallet for emergencies and told the owner that he would be back in about two hours to return the jack. In the meantime, the owner took the $100 bill to the auto parts store next door to pay for the part he had put on hold, which he needed to fix a car that a customer was coming to pick up in about an hour.

The parts store owner took the $100 bill to the grocery store that was next to his store and bought some meat for the company barbeque that evening. The grocery store immediately paid $100 to the butcher for the meat he cut for the store that day. The butcher then went directly to the farmer and paid $100 for the meat he bought on credit earlier that day. Now, the farmer went across town to the feed store to pay for the feed he needed for his cattle. The feed store owner paid $100 to the delivery truck driver for delivering the feed to his store.

The truck driver took the $100 to his doctor, as he had seen him the day before for not feeling well. The doctor then took the $100 to the town pharmacy to pay for the supplies he had purchased on credit. The pharmacy owner then took the $100 to the local auto repair shop to pay for the repairs that were just finished on her vehicle. Just then, the businessman arrived to return the jack and retrieve his $100 deposit.

This story is an example of how the velocity of a $100 bill moved in an economy and generated $1,000 in less than two hours. What happens if the money ends up under a mattress for safe keeping? On a larger scale, this is what banks do with the deposits we make. They, in turn, loan it out. Normally, the money loaned goes back to the bank in the form of a deposit, and the cycle repeats. Money is multiplied this way and helps an economy thrive. The economy is robust when the velocity is high and sluggish when the velocity is slow.

Stock Market (United States)

What is a bull market? What is a bear market? These terms are used to describe the U.S. stock market and the condition it is currently in. When the term bear market is used, it means the market is bearish and in a downward trend (bad). When the term bull market is used, it is the opposite and means the market is bullish and has an upward trend (good). I believe this has something to do with the 7,000-pound charging bull that has been at the New York Stock Exchange for many years. A trick I use to remember which one is which is to recall that bulls have horns and they point up!

What do you know about the derivative market? Why should you even care? On the surface, a normal person like you or me probably does not care. I want to change your mind on that if this is true. Let us start with a basic understanding of the term derivative. A derivative is a security with a price that is dependent upon or derived from one or more underlying assets. The derivative itself is a contract between two or more parties, based upon the asset or assets.

Did I lose you? I once heard a simple explanation—visualize an orange as an asset, and it is being traded on the market. Now, an orange has juice inside—the juice is a derivative of the orange. So, how can the juice be traded if the orange is being traded as a whole? Exactly. This is happening in so many asset classes. It seems as if the derivative market is just another way to facilitate a gambling addiction.

Of course, there is more to this explanation, but to the average person who does not invest, there is no need to go further, except to know why we need to know about it. And that reason is because of its size. In early 2020, the estimation of the derivative market was believed to be in excess of $1 quadrillion. That is 1,000 trillion. Or here's a visual: more than $1,000,000,000,000,000.00.

Commodities and assets are being traded, and derivatives of those assets are being traded as well. For example, let us go back to the orange and the juice. The orange is being traded, and it includes the juice. Then a derivative is created for the juice, and that is traded as well. Even though the juice is part of the orange. In other words, most derivatives are fake, and there is a market so deep in this that is over $1 quadrillion of nothing. Can anything go wrong here? Can you imagine a market this size betting (investing) on underlying assets? Marinate on that. I do not think anyone in an average financial position would be immune to some sort of financial injury if it were to be disrupted in any way.

Why are margin calls so dangerous? I will not get too deep into this, but it is very important for you to understand margins as they pertain to the stock market. Yes, you must be aware of this. An investor can increase their gains by buying securities on margin. And all this means is that the broker lends the investor money to purchase more shares. It is a loan, and the security (stock) is used as collateral. This works well for all when the market goes up, and everyone is happy because they are making money.

But what about when the market goes down? If the value of the share reaches a margin set by the broker, and it puts the broker's money at risk, the broker demands more money to be added to the investor's account, or they sell off the securities. So far this is straightforward, right? Now, remember, this was a loan, so would you think that the investor has the money to add? Probably not, and depending on the investor's position, they will try to preserve a portion of their portfolio and will end up selling this security or other securities within their portfolio to salvage the securities they desire to retain. This action, in turn, creates a sell off within the market.

Now, imagine the market is startled for whatever reason, and this is happening with tens of thousands of investors and brokers in a short span of time. Once this starts, there is no prediction when the market will stabilize. Just recently, in February through April of 2020, the world saw the fastest fall in global stock markets in financial history. Did you catch the word global? When a market crashes, businesses close, and people do not work. More businesses close, and more people do not work. The downward cycle continues until it hits bottom. This will affect you and me if we are not prepared, and this, my friend, is why you must know this stuff.

Banking

Is your money safe here? The banking system wants you to believe it is. These institutions promote a false sense of security by touting deposit insurance. Deposit insurance is an instrument for a depositor to have confidence and security in depositing their currency in their local bank. In the U.S., it is called the Federal Deposit Insurance Corporation (FDIC) and guarantees deposits up to $250,000. In Europe, it is called European Deposit Insurance Scheme (EIDS) and guarantees deposits up to 100,000 euro. In Brazil, it is called Credit Guarantee Fund (FGC) and guarantees deposits up to 250,000 real. These are just a few. I have met many people who keep money in the bank and believe that their deposits are safe and secure. But closely examine the details of this insurance. Apply the knowledge you have recently gained by reading this book. Now that you know how fragile our monetary system is, how safe is your money?

So, let us add a few more details. First, know that only a small fraction of money is set aside for a bank failure. And if a larger bank were to fail, such as Deutsche Bank or JP Morgan, could the insurance companies insure all their losses? These banks operate in the trillions of U.S. dollars. Second, since the insurance is limited, would they be able to cover everyone's losses? You are probably thinking, *Ummm, no.* Now I ask you, and be truthful, would you be on the top of the list to be repaid for your losses? My point to this is not to be naïve to the deceptions of the banks. If you have that much money sitting around, or perhaps you will in the future, this knowledge should be a consideration of your financial planning.

CHAPTER 15

WAKE UP

*"When plunder becomes a way of life, men create for themselves a
legal system that authorizes it and a moral code that glorifies it."*
—**Frédéric Bastiat**, French Economist, 1801-1850

Frédéric Bastiat was a French economist and was considered by his peers to be the most brilliant economic journalist who ever lived. The quote that opens this chapter almost exactly describes what I have been awakened to. As a beginning investor, I quickly noticed that our currency system in the United States was not what it seemed on the surface. Then, additional learning revealed that it was not just the U.S.—it is a global problem.

As I stated earlier, the person who has the gold, makes the rules. Never, ever forget this. We explored many topics that I originally had no idea about or just misunderstood. Like most folks, I assumed our economy was on the up-and-up. I hope this book has raised questions and provoked thought that will launch you on your own quest for a deeper understanding of the threat to our economy and that of the world.

Early in my research, there was this guy who had worked on my team, and since our helicopter assembly plant was closing, he had to sell his house and move away for another job. He boasted how he made

$100,000 on the sale of his home. I asked him what he was going to do with it. His reply was that he was going to do nothing. I was puzzled and asked for his reasoning. He told me that he wanted to see the amount (digits) in his bank account. I tried to explain to him that he was losing money, even if he was earning a mere one percent (or less), and he replied, "But I will still have $100,000 in my account." I tried to explain that inflation would reduce his purchase power over time, but he would not hear of it. It was more important to him to have the digits in his account.

I have encountered many people with this mindset and have come to expect to be surrounded by people like this. They do not want your help. What do you think he could have done? Of course, it all depends on each of our goals, but right away, perhaps purchasing a small percentage in gold or silver for starters. Perhaps investing in a rental property, or maybe just loaning the money out to achieve a better interest rate, to name a few. Of course, if he had bad debt, like credit card debt, he could pay that off as well.

You do not need to be a financial strategist or economist to understand your finances. It is your duty to know what is going on in the world so that you can react and plan for your present and future life. After learning some of the topics we covered in this book, you probably now see a light at the end of the tunnel you may find yourself in. The thing to consider is what kind of light is it: the headlight of a train, or is it sunshine at end of the tunnel? That is for you to figure out.

I have one more story to share from my time as a manager. I witnessed this scenario unfold many times with my elderly employees. I could never understand why people had to stay working past their retirement age, as many did. Unlike many in this world, the people I am talking about had great pensions but still needed to work. When I asked why they were not enjoying their golden years (70 years or older), they told me it was for the money or the health insurance. One of my guys was a hazard to himself, as we worked from dangerous heights. He started shaking so badly he almost fell. He did not have a plan other than to work until he died. It is never too late to change your plans. It is important to get educated about your finances and take action. The younger you are, the better off you will be. Do not be the seventy-five-year-old in a must-work-to-eat situation.

My final thought on the global economy is there is something on the horizon, and I have presented only probabilities, not certainties. The way I see it is that we all have become comfortable and accustomed to playing on a familiar board game, but I see an entirely new board game has started, and many players have already started on this new game. Is this digital currency? Perhaps the great reset? Soon, the old game will end, and there may not be any place for people to play on the new game. From the great reset to quantitative easing to interest rate reductions to Universal Basic Income, there is no shortage of what the bankers and the elites will do to save themselves. That is a certainty.

REMEMBER: The institutions and the elite have the gold and will not give up control for anyone (except for themselves). And that is why it is more important than ever to pay attention to what they are doing. Many experts will confess that the global economy should have crashed many years ago, yet it is still here. I am by no means claiming that it will be here forever, as no one knows what the bankers' next move will be. What is happening now is that the Federal Reserve Bank is purchasing a lot of assets with money created out of thin air. How long can this go on? Is it fair to us? Is it fair to the world? It is time that the world breaks free of this debt-based monetary system and starts a new system that is considered an honest money system. Your job is to figure out how you will fare going through the transition and how you are positioned financially on the other side.

CHAPTER 16

NOW WHAT?

"It is impossible for a man to learn
what he thinks he already knows."
— **Epictetus** (50-135) Greek Stoic Philosopher

What is this other side? Okay, this is how I see the monetary world. Imagine that the entire global population is playing this board game. We all have our pieces, and we are trying to move them around each other to get to the… end? This game is so intense for us, and we are only paying attention to our immediate surroundings on the board. This is a game that has been played for a very long time, and, as a matter of fact, it is all we know how to play.

Now, the owners of the game cannot keep this old game going for much longer and have created a new board game, and they are now setting up the pieces and rewriting the rules. The people paying attention to them see this new game being set up, and they are beginning to prepare for this new game. Unfortunately, most people of the world are not seeing the new game set up and are so distracted trying to win in the old game. I believe that old board and all the pieces will be gone. The old game will be over. Then there will be a mad rush for everyone to join in on the new game, and there will not be enough pieces for everyone to play. I believe when this happens, people stand the risk of losing a lot, if not everything.

But here you are. You lifted your head up from your play, read this book, and looked around. You are seeing the setup of the new game. My intention was to share with you what I have learned and what they want to keep you distracted from seeing. I am going to state the obvious here: in any game, there are winners and losers. Now, I also realize that we all are at different starting points when it comes to our finances. The cool thing is, knowledge is power, and I believe if you learn and invest in yourself first, you can get to the other side in a good way. You may find yourself looking at money and currency differently as your knowledge and wisdom increases.

As for how to implement all the new things you've learned, I do not want to give you any specific instructions to "do this" or "do that," as we all have different skills and need to capitalize on each of our unique qualities that God has blessed us with. So, here are some of the experts I trust and recommend you check out to start honing your new financial knowledge. Wayne Gretzky, one of the greatest hockey players, said, "A good hockey player plays where the puck is. A great hockey player plays where the puck is going to be." Let's have this mindset.

I recommend starting with Robert Kiyosaki. He is the author of *Rich Dad, Poor Dad,* and this book, in my opinion, should be required reading for everyone. There is so much to learn from him, but the most important to me was to change my mindset. His book explains that the way we think can lead us to either wealth or poverty. He is committed to helping us and has numerous YouTube videos, and he does a *Rich Dad* radio show that goes deeper with experts on the topics we introduced in this book. You can discover more at www.richdad.com.

To gain an in-depth understanding on the banking system and current investing, I recommend checking out George Gammon from the *Rebel Capitalist Show*. His team has a YouTube channel and has numerous videos in a relatable format using three simple steps to explain his topic. George has this incredible way of breaking down complex systems or topics for us to understand. You can find him at www.georgegammon.com.

Many websites have interview-style lessons, and they cover a wide variety of financial topics. My two go-to websites are:

1. **Daniela Cambone** of Stansberry Research. Daniela is a very seasoned and experienced investor and speaks with the top people of the financial industry. The YouTube channel is *Stansberry Research*.

2. **David Lin** of Kitco News. David is also a topnotch interviewer and well informed. He provides an engaging and valuable experience with the top people in the industry. The YouTube channel is *Kitco NEWS*.

Precious metals can be a bit mysterious, but you can get more understanding from these fine teachers:

1. **Lynette Zang**: She is the Chief Market Analyst for ITM Trading. She offers her vast experience of the economy and provides strategies with the use of precious metals. She has personally experienced financial crisis and crashes that have allowed her to express what is happening in today's market from a survivor's point of view. Her YouTube channel is *ITM Trading, Inc.*

2. **Peter Schiff**: He is the Chief Economist and Global Strategist of Euro Pacific Capital. He provides his experience of gold and the current economy through his own *The Peter Schiff Show*. His YouTube channel is *Peter Schiff*.

3. **Mike Maloney**: He is the founder of Goldsilver.com and has authored books such as *Hidden Secrets of Money* and *Guide to Investing in Gold and Silver*. He does many economic updates on YouTube, and I find them to be very helpful. His YouTube channel is *GoldSilver (w/Mike Maloney)*.

To learn more about the central banks and the Federal Reserve Bank, I have found **Danielle DiMartino Booth**, CEO of Quill Intelligence, to be helpful. She authored a book called *Fed Up*. She is a former Federal Reserve Bank insider advisor, and she gives a unique perspective of the inner workings of central banks. Her YouTube channel is *Danielle DiMartino Booth*.

On to cryptocurrencies. There are so many resources available, but the most helpful I have discovered are the following:

1. A great how-to person for all things crypto, from primary coins to altcoins, is **Nate Martin**. He hosts a channel called *99Bitcoins* on YouTube, and you can get a three-minute video of virtually any topic regarding cryptocurrencies.

In the late 1970s, I remember a television commercial for a broker called E.F. Hutton. The tagline was, "When E.F. Hutton talks, people listen." The visual of this was that everybody stopped what they were doing to hear what this broker said. It was a very popular commercial in the U.S. Just like E.F. Hutton back in the '70s, there are some names today that you can trust and should listen to. I have found these people to be well rounded about the topics we have covered in this book, and they will be able to lead you further into any area they address. So, when they speak, you should listen.

1. **Ray Dalio**: Billionaire hedge fund manager of the world's largest

hedge fund, Bridgewater Associates. He is sought after for many interviews and has a lot of information to offer.

2. **Ron Paul**: Former U.S. congressman and an advocate for sound money. He hosts a daily show called *The Liberty Report* and can be viewed on YouTube.

3. **Jim Rogers**: He is probably the humblest investor I have learned from. He is informative on current financial events and trends and what actions to take in response.

4. **James Rickards**: He is an author and writes books that have an uncanny way of taking today's events and predicting where we will be in the future. He has a wide range of experience from being a lawyer, holding senior positions with Citibank, and serving as an advisor to the Department of Defense regarding global financial issues.

Here we are at the end. These sites and names are not all inclusive, and I assure you, the more you seek, the more you will discover. Most of the experts listed here do sell a service or a product, and I am not endorsing them for that reason. I only seek to lead you to some people who I have found helpful in general or for specific topics.

I have also created a Telegram page for the book for readers like you to connect with questions or information to share. This is a rapidly changing environment, and many news topics are posted here as well to help keep you up to date. You can subscribe for free at: https://t.me/moneyplainandsimple. I am looking forward to connecting with you!

In the U.S. Air Force, our official song goes like this: "Off we go into the wild blue yonder." In a sense, that is where I hope your thoughts and dreams have shifted as well. Your personal roadmap to navigate the mess ahead of us is now being drawn in your mind, and I wish you success. Perhaps you can teach others. Spread the lessons I shared with you and help as many who have ears to hear. Thank you for reading my book, and may God bless you.

CHAPTER 17

2023 AND BEYOND

*"Learn how to see. Realize that everything
connects to everything else."*
—**Leonardo da Vinci** (1452-1519) Painter, Draughtsman,
engineer, scientist, theorist, sculptor, and architect

Making it through 2022 was challenging for most people as they watched interest rates rise, equities decline, and prices for the basics you need like housing, food, utilities, and gas skyrocket. Most of us are too busy to study why this is all happening and have become reactionary with managing our finances. When you are in survival mode, flipping into being proactive seems out of reach. In the U.S.A., most Americans only see what is happening in their own lives and do not pay attention to what is going on in the rest of the world. Keeping up with world events can be overwhelming, especially when you are barely able to keep your head above water.

Some people still believe that the U.S.A. is the wealthiest nation in the world. The reality is that by the end of 2022, 63% of Americans were living paycheck to paycheck. Add to this 'wealth' deception, the reported personal savings went from all-time highs in 2021 to very low lows by the end of 2022. Meanwhile, credit card debt has increased to all-time highs.

What all of this is signaling to me is that people are financially struggling. The question is ***How much longer is this situation going to continue?***

That question would be easier to answer if this problem were just isolated to one country, but it is not. We are looking at a global issue. From world reserve currency status, economic sanctions, the war in Ukraine, and rumors of wars and more pestilences, the possibility of a new world order is real. At the very least, challenges to the existing order are happening. My intent in this chapter is to identify for you what *may* come and how these shifts can possibly affect you. I am going to stay on the *Plain & Simple* level and encourage you to study the following issues further as they develop.

Because of our economic connections around the globe, the things that can be brought to your doorstep may surprise you. Believe me, there is a lot going on, and once you see how it is unfolding, you can start your own plan of action to protect yourself and your family.

Inflation

We covered this topic earlier in the book: what it is and how it affects all of us. We also covered how inflation is combatted by the Federal Reserve Bank to bring stability to the U.S. dollar while keeping unemployment as low as possible. In 2021, the U.S. started to see the effects of inflation with higher consumer prices in everything the average person needs. At the time, there appeared to be enough in savings to accommodate these increases. However, another important thing to note is that there are other inputs to inflation.

Plain and simple pricing is derived from supply and demand. Too much supply and low demand brings lower prices, and conversely too little supply and high demand brings higher prices. Agreed? So, in regards of inflating the money supply, and not increasing the supply of goods and services, then prices will go up as there is too much money chasing too few goods. Compound this with the fact that supply chains break down or just become more expensive. That too will cause consumer prices to rise.

In 2022, the U.S. Congress enacted the Inflation Reduction Act, H.R. 5376. We won't get into the details of this bill except for the intention of it is to combat inflation as the title suggests. The U.S. Congress appropriated $437 billion dollars to spend into the economy. If we do a quick analysis of this bill, we know that any money the government spends is usually borrowed. Typically to borrow this much will ultimately come from the Fed, which creates the reserves. So now, more money is introduced to the aggregate money supply, which does what? Yep, inflates the money supply. Then we have more money chasing goods, and to add insult to injury, the American people must repay this loan with more taxes. One of the major steps to curb high prices is to become fiscally responsible and that must start with the government and its spending habits.

Recession? Depression?

What is a recession? A good place to start a plain and simple discussion may be with some definitions.

- A recession is defined as a prolonged downturn in economic activity usually identified as two consecutive quarters of negative gross domestic product (GDP).
- GDP is simply the total monetary value of all the finished goods and services produced within a country's borders in a specific period.
- A depression is a dramatic downturn in economic activity. They are usually identified as extended recessions.

President Ronald Reagan described it this way: "Recession is when your neighbor loses his job. Depression is when you lose yours."

Now, recall one of the Fed's goal is to maintain the US dollar purchasing power. Recall that this non-government group of bankers accomplishes this by governing the amount of money in the system and raising and lowering the federal funds rate. In the US, inflation reached 40-year highs by the end of 2022, and the Fed has been responding as I described. The Federal Reserve, which most of us never even think about, has increased the federal funds rate at the fastest pace ever. They also have been reducing the money supply, but that amount is still above pre-2020 levels. The CPI has inched down to just over 7% year-over-year. Oops, I think I geeked out on you a little bit!

Back to Plain & Simple; The Fed is predicting more rate hikes as it needs to get the CPI back down to 2%. The Fed simultaneously tightens the money supply, removing liquidity from the economy. This move will make it more difficult for companies to stay in business as many have depended on cheap and easy money for around a decade.

Many experts note that a recession looms in 2023 as liquidity dries up and people lose jobs. As jobs are lost, bills are not paid and so starts the spiral downward. It does not help when you hear the Federal Reserve Chairman J. Powell warn in a speech, he delivered in August 2022 regarding the Fed rate hikes will bring *"some pain to households and businesses."*

Ukraine and Russia Invasion/War

The Russian invasion of Ukraine in February 2022 has created so much division of people and nations around the world. If you examine which countries support and which are against, you will begin to see the alliances forming between the eastern and western countries of the world. Many people do not understand why this happened, and some do not know that there is even a war going on. I am not getting into the politics of this, but we cannot ignore the fact of how much money is being sent in support of Ukraine from the USA and allies. According to a United States Congressional Inspector General report, the U.S. has sent $113 billion in support of their defense against Russia in 2022. The war doesn't look like it will not end anytime soon and there will likely be more aid sent in 2023. What does this mean to the average American? More money created, and yes, you guessed it, more inflation, resulting in higher prices and higher taxes.

What else has occurred due to the invasion? I'm glad you asked! Let's begin with sanctions. Yes, the US has economically sanctioned Russia, seizing financial assets of the nation and its citizens. Private yachts and aircraft were seized as well as bank accounts frozen. Again, I am not trying to sway an opinion of what is right or wrong but present the case of incentives to remove themselves from the US dollar hegemony. I will cover more of this in a later paragraph. Also, the other superpower nation, The Peoples Republic of China is watching and planning as well. China is looking long and hard at Taiwan. China knows it too will be sanctioned by the US if it proceeds with a military operation.

Remember the supply input I mentioned earlier? That too is impacted primarily in the western nations. Mostly in Europe, countries are experiencing a dramatic slowdown in oil and natural gas that was provided to them by Russia. Because of their role in sanctioning Russia, they have reduced their energy dependence from Russia. Regardless of who is refusing to deliver or take delivery, the result is the same. The input prices to the supply side are rapidly increasing. If the war is not resolved soon, this supply input will impact the western countries. As you can imagine, higher input prices will result in higher product prices. Why only 'west'? I will show you later.

ESG

No, this is not the thing you check in your food if you have high blood pressure. ESG is short for "Environmental Social Governance." That sounds like fun, doesn't it? This is where the elitists are taking us, under the guise of "Climate Change," Recall earlier the WEF statement: "you will own nothing and like it"? Again, not a topic to argue here, I merely want to show you what is on the horizon as you will be hearing this more and more in the near future. You may be in support of these policies, because who does not want to save the planet? Well, open your wallets and pocketbooks as this price tag is going to hurt. Warren Buffet's partner, Charlie Munger once said: "Show me the incentive and I will show you the outcome," There are trillions of dollars committed to this, and that my friend is an attractive incentive.

FedNow

Coming to a country near you! What is it? Well, this is what I wrote earlier about CBDCs (Central Bank Digital Currency). This is the Federal Reserve Bank version. It will never happen you say? Well guess what? They already tested this system in late 2022 and are planning on launching this program in mid-2023. It is aimed initially to make instant payments and deposits. Then, the FedNow Service will be released in phases and additional features and service enhancements will be introduced over time. Other central banks around the world will follow suit too. Get UpToDate information from the www.federalreserve.gov website.

Oh the fun! They can have a whole new monetary system, with programs like: programable currency (your purchases will no longer be private); control over your savings (like they did to the Canadian donors to the trucker protesters in 2021 by freezing their accounts); and immediate tax collection to name a few. The central banks will be in total control of the money supply. Remember Kissinger's quote at the beginning of chapter 9.

BRICS+

This is probably the most important acronym you should familiarize yourself with for the near future and its strength is rising faster than most have expected. What is it? BRICS+ stands for: **B**razil, **R**ussia, **I**ndia, **C**hina and **S**outh Africa. The plus is for all the nations that are applying to join this alliance. To do what? To form an alliance of emerging nations to counter the west economically to include a challenge to the U.S. dollar hegemony as the only world reserve currency. The sanctions the US placed on Russia and that may possibly be placed later on China are accelerants to launch their own reserve currency that is backed by gold and a basket of other commodities. They have already announced their intentions of implementing this as early as 2023. The more the west sanctions the east, the more the east disconnects from the west.

On to the 'plus'! These are the nations that have submitted applications as a BRICS expansion. As of November 2022, they are Algeria, Argentina, and Iran. Saudi Arabia, Turkey, Egypt, Indonesia and Afghanistan are expected to apply and others such as Kazakhstan, Nicaragua, Nigeria, Senegal, Thailand, and the United Arab Emirates are exploring membership. If accepted, the new proposed BRICS members would create an entity with a GDP 30% larger than the U.S., over 50% of the global population and in control of 60% of global gas reserves. Reference www.silkroadbriefing.com

Do you remember the 'petro dollar'? That agreement the U.S. and Saudi Arabia had that their oil is priced in U.S. dollars? This is important as it kept the demand for dollars worldwide and gave it its value to a currency that should be worthless. Due to this arrangement, the U.S.

enjoyed the privilege of printing the money it needed, when it needed it. What Saudi Arabia wanted in return was military protection. Fast forward to the summer of 2021, the Russians were able to convince the Saudis that they would now protect them, especially after their confidence in the U.S.A. was shaken due to the Afghanistan withdrawal. This move also gave the Chinese confidence to strike a deal with Saudi Arabia to begin selling oil in RMB (Chinese Yuan). Remember, the eastern nations are working together to get around using the U.S. dollar as it has been weaponized via sanctions. Will the new reserve currency be called the "Petro Yuan"?

Another indicator of something to unfold is the stock piling of gold reserves by central banks. The World Gold Council (WGC) reported that purchases of gold is the highest in late 2022 in over 55 years with Russia and China leading the way. As a reminder, the US dollar was backed by gold until 1971. Is this part of the plan to back the BRICS+ reserve currency? Hopefully this will paint the picture of the East and West divide as it seems the west has become mostly consumers while the east has become producers.

Take Away

Whew! That is a lot to digest! I hope I did not frighten you. I learned a while ago, *Be prepared, not scared.* Pay attention to these topics and watch them unfold. Learn more about them and how they can affect you and your family. I am going to list what I see coming and what to expect. You will need to decide how to prepare.

The Fed is seeking to reduce the CPI, they combat this by raising interest rates and reducing the money supply. The US government is counterproductive by increased spending. More spending equals more inflation and higher costs. The Fed will be forced to raise interest rates more.

Raising interest rates will end an era of cheap money. You should anticipate the stock market will drop if this cycle continues and banks fail.

$ide Note: In mid-March, the first wave of bank failures began and the stock trading of at least four banks was halted as their stocks were in a volatile freefall. This was due to three banks that failed the week prior, one of them was the 16th largest in the U.S.A. As we know, all FDIC insured banks insure all deposits up to $250,000. For this particular bank, 90% of all depositors had more than the insured amount. The total was about $210 billion in one bank! Guess what the depositors were getting (at first) yes, the insured amount. This woke up the nation and the beginning of bank runs ensued on other banks. Yes, this is already happening in the U.S.A.! Would you believe that this first wave of bank failures was deemed 'too big to fail' (sound familiar?) by the U.S. Government and the Federal Reserve Bank and decided to aid the FDIC in guaranteeing the deposits 100%. The president of the United States even gave a statement to assure all Americans of the security of the American banking system in hopes to restore confidence. They really do not want you to know what 'fiat currency' means as this BandAid won't work without confidence in our currency. Did the government just set precedence over all deposits? Where did the currency come from? I know, you already know that they created it out of thin air. Oh, what is that you say? "Expect more inflation!" Wow, you get it! I am so proud of you. Now to be fair to the government as they announced that the taxpayer will not be liable for this as they will sell off all the banking assets to recoup the not a bailout bailout. We shall see later how that worked out.

If this continues, expect a recession. That will result in high unemployment, car repossessions, home foreclosures and a reduction in overall spending. Governments have to make a choice to create more money or practice austerity. They normally choose to print. Printing means even higher prices.

It seems the central banks want a collapse in order to usher in the Fed Now system. The Fed Now will not be well received once people begin to wake up to this. At the risk of sounding conspiratorial, I would not be surprised if the financial system crashes and this is offered as a solution. This is the mode of operations now a days, using the Hegelian dialect as I described earlier. The population will beg for financial relief.

Expect the US dollar to share the stage with another reserve currency. What will this mean? When will it happen? One would think overnight, but the economy is so large that it may take years for everything to play out. That does not mean that you can go back to business as usual. You now know more than 99 percent of the population in U.S. You never should prepare for a storm while you are in it. Get ready now for what's coming.

ACKNOWLEDGEMENTS

To my talented book coach Danielle Anderson, who took the time to guide me as a first-time author putting together this book. All the editing and coaching was invaluable to making this book a reality. I thank you for keeping me on track while always sharing my vision to reach our readers. You challenged me in many ways to make this topic understandable to all.

To Echo Montgomery Garrett for investing her expertise and talent to guide and publish *Money Plain & Simple*. I am sure our paths crossed through a divine intervention when you and my wife Adriana met on a plane in Minneapolis. We were praying about next steps for the book and were on the verge of self-publishing. Our prayers were answered through the two of you meeting and ultimately us working together. I am forever grateful for you and Lucid House Publishing for taking a chance on this book. You took me, as an author, and this book to a level I could only dream of. Because of you, this book will reach and help more people than I could ever imagined. Thank you so much for everything.

ABOUT THE AUTHOR

Steven J. Spence is a retired US Air Force veteran, airline mechanic, aircraft builder and an owner of a real estate rental investment company. Spence grew up with a single mom, who immigrated from Germany with her American military husband only to find herself alone with two young sons in the wake of a divorce. With no role models, he had no understanding about how to build his financial future. Throughout his military career and airline career he was led to teach and has traveled all over the world speaking to groups on airline safety. He is passionate about helping others. Now a successful entrepreneur, Spence focuses on financial literacy as it relates to the ordinary person and has been quoted in national media about the currency crisis. He and his wife Adriana have two daughters, Shannon and Rachel, a son, Lucas, and one grandson, Julian. He resides in Wellington, Florida.

To connect with Steven J. Spence, read his blog, or book him for a speaking engagement, please visit: moneyplainandsimple.com

INDEX